## Young People's Science Encyclopedia

## An

Anise
Annealing
Annelida
Annual
Annual rings
Anode
Antacid
Antarctica
Anteater
Antelope
Antenna
Anthropology
Antibiotics
Antibody
Antidote
Antifreeze
Antimatter
Antimony
Antiseptic
Ants

## Ap

Apatite
Ape
Aphid
Apogee
Apoplexy
Appendix
Apple
Apricot

## Aq

Aquaculture
Aquarium
Aquila

## Ar

Arachnida
Arboretum
Arborvitae
Arc
Archaeopteryx
Archeology
Archeozoic Era
Archimedes
Archipelago
Arctic
Area
Argon
Argonaut
Arid
Aries
Aristotle
Arithmetic
Armadillo
Armature
Arnica
Arrowroot
Arsenic
Arteriosclerosis
Artery
Arthritis

Arthropoda
Artichoke
Artificial
   respiration
Artiodactyla

## As

Asbestos
Ascaris
Ash
Asia
Asparagus
Aspen
Asphalt
Asphyxia
Aspirin
Assaying
Assimilation
Astatine
Aster
Asteroid
Asthma
Astigmatism
Astragalus
Astringent
Astrolabe
Astrology
Astronaut
Astronautics
Astronomy
Astrophysics

## At

Atavism
Athlete's foot
Atmosphere
Atoll
Atom
Atrophy
Atropine

## Au

Audubon, John James
Auk
Auriga
Aurora borealis
Australia
Autogiro
Automation
Automobile
Autonomic
   nervous system
Autotomy
Autumnal equinox

## Av

Avalanche
Aviation
Avocado
Avocet

## Az

Azalea

# YOUNG PEOPLE'S
# SCIENCE ENCYCLOPEDIA

Edited by the Staff of
NATIONAL COLLEGE OF EDUCATION, Evanston, Illinois

## ASSOCIATE EDITORS

HELEN J. CHALLAND, B.E., M.A., Ph.D.
Chairman, Division of Natural Sciences
National College of Education,
Evanston, Illinois

DONALD A. BOYER, B.S., M.S., Ph.D.
Science Education Consultant, Winnetka
Public Schools, Winnetka, Illinois
Science, National College of Education

## EDITORIAL CONSULTANTS
## ON THE STAFF OF NATIONAL COLLEGE OF EDUCATION

Elizabeth R. Brandt, B.A., M.Ed.
Eugene B. Cantelupe, B.A., M.F.A., Ph.D.
John H. Daugherty, B.S., M.A.
Irwin K. Feinstein, B.S., M.A., Ph.D.
Mary Gallagher, A.B., M.A., Ph.D.
Beatrice S. Garber, A.B., M.S., Ph.D.
Hal S. Galbreath, B.S. Ed., M.S.
Arthur J. Hannah, B.S., M.Ed., Ed.D.

Robert R. Kidder, A.B., M.A., Ph.D.
Jean C. Kraft, B.S., M.A., Ph.D.
Elise P. Lerman, B.A., B.F.A., M.F.A.
Mary M. Lindquist, B.A., M.A., Ph.D.
Mary-Louise Neumann, A.B., B.S.L.S.
Lavon Rasco, B.A., M.A., Ph.D.
Bruce Allen Thale, B.S.Ed., M.S.Ed.
Fred R.Wilkins, Jr., B.A., M.Ed., Ph.D.

## SPECIAL SUBJECT AREA CONSULTANTS

Krafft A. Ehricke, B.A.E., H.L.D.
Benjamin M. Hair, A.B., M.D.
Charles B. Johnson, B.S., M.A., M.S.
Raymond J. Johnson, B.B.A., M.Ed.

H. Kenneth Scatliff, M.D.
Eleanor S. Segal, M.D.
Paul P. Sipiera, B.A., M.S.
Ray C. Soliday, B.A., B.S., M.A. (Deceased)

Don Dwiggins, Aviation Editor

## THE STAFF

Project Director        Rudolph A. Hastedt
Project Editor          M. Frances Dyra
Senior Editor           Jim Hargrove
Editorial Assistant     Janet Zelasko

# Young People's
# SCIENCE
## Encyclopedia

*Edited by the Staff of*

**NATIONAL COLLEGE OF EDUCATION**

*Evanston, Illinois*

## Volume 2/An-Az

 CHILDRENS PRESS

CHICAGO

Photographs

Page 2:   Skylab space station (NASA)

Page 3:   *Top to Bottom:*
          Wheatfield (U.S.D.A. Photo)
          Technician capping Abbokinase (Abbott Laboratories)
          Spider (Macmillan Science Company)
          View of Earth (NASA)
          Space Shuttle (NASA)
          Bahama coral reef (Macmillan Science Company)

Cover:    Saturn V (NASA)
          Space Shuttle (Rockwell International)
          Queensland Koala (San Diego Zoo)

Library of Congress Catalog Card Number: 67-17925

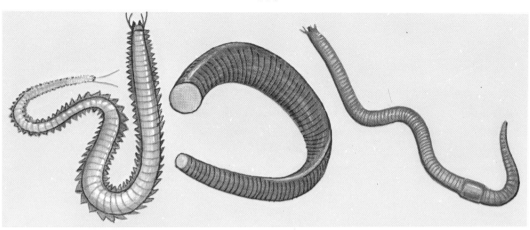

ANNELIDA

**Anise** (ANN-iss) Anise is a small herb with seeds that have a licorice taste. It is an annual plant belonging to the PARSLEY family. It grows 2 feet (.61 meters) high. The small flowers may be yellow or white. The brown fruit is coated with stubby hairs.

Anise is native to the Mediterranean region but is also grown in many areas of Europe, Asia and South America. One variety, the *star* or *Chinese anise,* is a small evergreen grown less widely, mainly in the Far East.

The essential oil (*anethole*) makes up 85% of the seed. This is distilled out and used in cosmetics and medicinal preparations. *Anisette* is a liqueur made from this herb. The seed is used in flavoring called *aniseed.*          H. J. C.

**Annealing** Annealing is a process of heating and cooling materials, such as metals or glass, to improve their qualities of hardness, brittleness, strength, and general workability. Annealing also relieves internal *stress* to assure better performance of the material in its finished product.          H. P. O.
SEE ALSO: STEEL

**Annelida** (uh-NE-luh-duh) The annelids are true worms. They form a large group living in salt water, fresh water, and on land. Unlike the other large group of true worms, the round-worms (Nematodes), the annelids are ringed or segmented. The rings are not merely depressions in the outer body wall but they continue into the inside of the body. The EARTHWORM, the sandworm, and the LEECH belong to the phylum Annelida.

In many ways, annelids are organized like freight trains. A freight train is really a long line of connected railroad cars, pulled by an engine. Each car is a separate part of the train, carrying its own load. But the cars are useless, as freight cars, unless they are connected to one another and to the engine. The engine is useless, unless it has freight cars to pull. The engine and the cars must work together to carry freight. Annelids, like trains, are made up of separate sections. Each ring is a separate part of the worm. These sections are divided by a thin wall or partition, just as the cars of the train are closed off from one another by two end walls. Annelids have a front and a rear end, just as the train has an engine and a caboose. The head moves first and the rest of the body follows. When a train goes around a curve, the cars are able to turn separately. It is an advantage for a worm to have a body built in sections, because each section can move separately and can perform special duties.

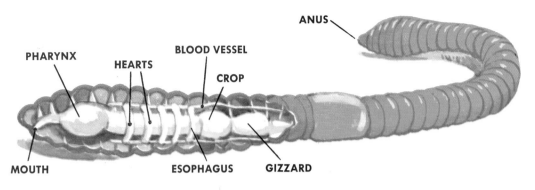

The Latin word *anellus* means ring. Annelids are members of a large phylum of ringed or segmented worms, which differ in size, location, and feeding habits. Included are both tiny worms, used as food for pet fish, as well as giant earthworms, which live in the tropics and grow to 11 feet (3.35 meters) in length. While the tube and sand-worms live in burrows along the ocean, the earthworms live in moist soils all over the world. Burrowing worms swallow great amounts of sand and soil, from which they extract decaying plant and animal matter. Parasitic worms, like the leeches, feed on blood by attaching themselves to the bodies of fish and other vertebrates. With their suckers, they are able to extract three times their own weight in blood, which they store as food for several months.

The body of the annelid is simple in structure. There are two tubes, a small, hollow, digestive tube, inserted into a large outer tube. The tubes are joined at the mouth on the first segment and at the anus on the last segment. Between the tubes, there is a space called the body cavity or *coelom,* which is filled with a fluid. The coelom is divided into compartments by the thin partitions between the rings or segments. Thus the fluid is confined within the segment. Contained in the thick outer tube, are two types of muscles. Circular muscles, which go around the body, contract to make the body longer and thinner. Longitudinal muscles, which run the length of the body, contract to make it shorter and thicker. The outer tube is covered with a *cuticle* which prevents the body from drying and allows for exchange of gases in respiration.

Among worms, annelids are unique, since a few have paired feet for locomotion. Extending from the sides of each segment, are either fleshy lobes, called *parapodia,* or tufts of bristles, called *setae,* or both. The feet beat like paddles to propel the worm; the bristles anchor the body to the ground.

Simple transportation systems are present. The nervous and circulatory systems run the length of the body. The nervous system consists of a dorsal brain and ventral nerve cord. The circulatory system is a closed circuit of branching blood vessels which propel the red blood by wave-like contractions (*peristalsis*) and prevent back-flow by a system of valves. Excretory funnels, the *nephridia,* in almost each segment, remove wastes from the blood and coelomic fluid. Reproductive organs are found in several anterior segments. Some species of annelids have separate males and females; others are hermaphroditic—both male and female in one animal. Some annelid eggs hatch into larva before they develop into adults.

Annelids are really advanced worms. Due to the presence of segments and appendages, these animals have achieved great control of body movements.       E. P. L.

SEE ALSO: ANIMAL; ANIMALS, CLASSIFICATION OF; NEMATHELMINTHES; PLATYHELMINTHES

**Annual** Plants are sometimes grouped according to how long they live. Annuals go through their entire life cycle in one year or season and then die. Biennials need two years to go from seed to seed. Perennials live for more than two years.

Annual plants begin as a seed that produces the vegetative and reproductive parts—roots, stem, leaves, flowers, and fruit. Before the season ends, new seeds form. The length of the life cycle of annuals varies from a few weeks to a full twelve months.     H.J.C.

SEE ALSO: PLANT

**Annual rings** Annual rings are the dark and light colored rings that can be seen when a tree is cut through the trunk. The age of the tree can be told by the rings. A light ring grows each spring and a dark one grows each summer and fall. Too little sunlight and moisture, injury, or age of the tree sometimes causes the annual rings to vary in width.

Annual rings are formed by living cells just inside the bark of the tree. These cells serve as a transportation system from the roots to all parts of the plant. Spring cells are usually larger than those grown in summer, and lighter in appearance.                    I.H.S.

SEE ALSO: CAMBIUM, PHLOEM, TREE, VASCULAR TISSUES, XYLEM

**Anode** The anode is the positive ELECTRODE by which an electric current enters a conductor. The conductor may be a liquid, a gas or a solid. The anode may be a terminal post as in a storage battery, a prong as in a radio or television tube, or a plate of impure copper as in the electrolytic refining of copper.

The anode may be the positively charged copper strip of a wet cell or the positive electrode of a television picture tube.

The anode is always positively charged, and the CATHODE is negatively charged. This is why the anode attracts the negatively charged ions or *anions*. It is at the anode that the anions give up their electrons and become oxidized.                    I.K.F.

SEE ALSO: ELECTROLYSIS, IONIZATION

**Anopheles** see Malaria, Mosquito

**Anorexia nervosa** (an-uh-REK-see-uh nur-VOH-suh) Anorexia nervosa is a condition in which a person refuses to eat enough food to remain healthy. It usually begins during times of mental stress. Victims often believe they are overweight, even after they have become dangerously thin. With prompt medical care, it can usually be permanently or temporarily cured.

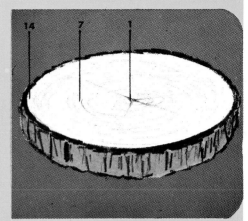

✳ **THINGS TO DO**

**HOW OLD IS A TREE?**

1    Secure a cross-section of a tree which has been cut down in the neighborhood.
2    Sand the surface until it is very smooth. Brush on clear shellac or varnish to bring out the "grain" in the wood.
3    Starting from the center (the first year's growth) count a light and dark band as one year. Notice how some bands are wider than others.
4    What would cause the wider bands? How old was the tree when you were born, when you started to school?

Teenaged girls are the most common victims of anorexia nervosa. The disease is often combined with another disorder known as *bulimia*. People suffering from bulimia sometimes eat large amounts of food and then force themselves to VOMIT. Some sufferers of anorexia nervosa recover without medical assistance. About ten percent die from starvation.                    J.H.

SEE ALSO: MALNUTRITION, NUTRITION, VITAMIN DEFICIENCY

**Antacid** An antacid is a chemical substance which lessens the amount of acid in the stomach either by neutralizing or by absorbing it.

SEE: ACIDS AND BASES, DIGESTIVE SYSTEM

**Antagonist** see Muscle system

**Antarctic current** see Currents, ocean

**Little America, the base established by Admiral Richard E. Byrd in 1928, was revisited by him in the sailing ship *Bear of Oakland* in 1939**

**Antarctica** Antarctica is the only continent of the earth that is uninhabited. Teams of scientists from many different nations are the only visitors. It is the southernmost continent. Its area is over 5 million square miles (13 million square kilometers), almost twice the size of the continental United States.

Before 1900, people knew little about Antarctica except the shape of some of its coastline. Captain James Cook, a British explorer, first reached the area about 1774. Some time later, a Russian named Bellingshausen discovered two islands and the sea which bears his name. The long, finger-like PENINSULA which extends westward from Antarctica was named after the American explorer Nathaniel Palmer, who discovered it, though he had no idea that Antarctica was a continent. In 1823, James Weddell found a sea north of Palmer Peninsula. It is now named for him. It wasn't until 1840 that Charles Wilkes identified the area as a continent. He had followed the coast for about 1000 miles (1609.34 kilometers). A year later James Clark Ross of Britain discovered the famous Ross Ice Shelf. From then until the turn of the century, new knowledge concerning Antarctica was very slight.

In the twentieth century extensive expeditions have been undertaken to learn more about this vast continent. Despite these attempts, over a million square miles (2.6 million square kilometers) are yet to be explored. Ernest Shackleton of Great Britain attempted to reach the South Pole in 1908-1909 but failed. On December 14, 1911, ROALD AMUNDSEN was the first man to reach the South Pole. A month later on January 18, Robert Scott, an Englishman, arrived there. In 1928 Hubert Wilkins was the first man to fly over the Pole in an airplane. In 1929 Admiral RICHARD E. BYRD established, off the Bay of Whales on the Ross Ice Shelf, an outpost called Little America. On November 29 of that year he, too, flew over the Pole. Byrd led several expeditions to Antarctica—1934-35, 1940, and 1946-47. In 1935 he was surprised to learn that part of the ice shelf had dropped off into the ocean. Presently, Antarctic research is encouraged by the National Science Foundation and continued by the United States Antarctic Research Program's Operation Deep Freeze. During the Antarctic summer months, McMurdo Station is populated by over 1,000 scientists and support personnel.

There is much evidence to support the idea that Antarctica has had a tropical to subtropical climate in the geological past. About one hundred million years ago its climate was similar to the climate that California has today. Vegetation that grows only in a tropical climate then covered Antarctica. It was this vegetation that formed the extensive layers of coal found there today. Also, fossils of animals that thrive in a warm climate have been found. Today Antarctica has an ice cap climate, having low temperatures all year. Temperatures in the winter reach −80°F (−62.2°C) near

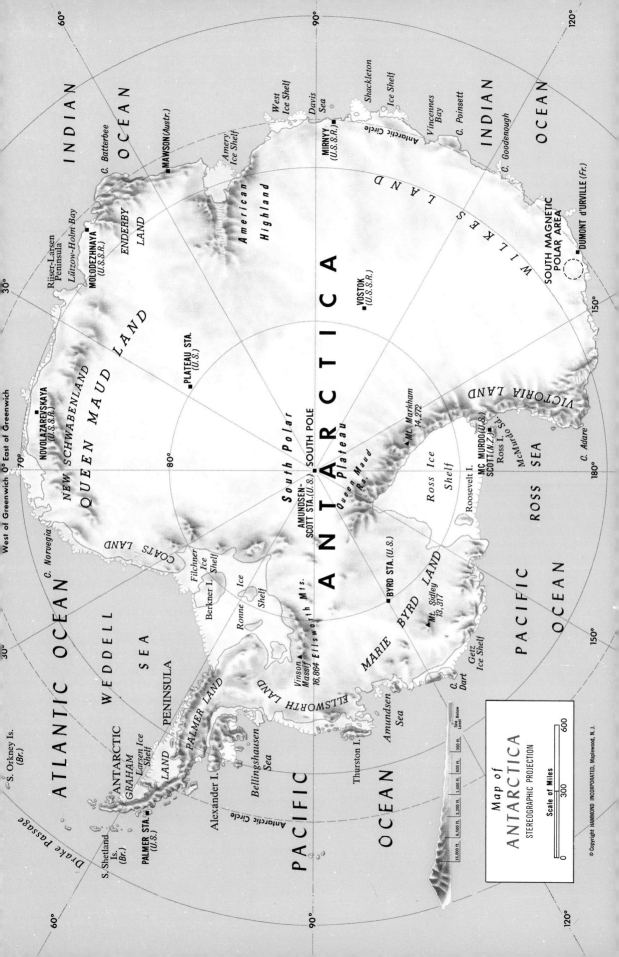

Map of
ANTARCTICA
STEREOGRAPHIC PROJECTION

Scale of Miles
0        300        600

© Copyright HAMMOND INCORPORATED, Maplewood, N.J.

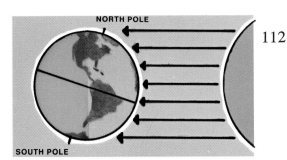

At the south pole the sun does not shine for three months of the year.

the coast and $-100°F$ ($-73.3°C$) inland. In the interior the temperatures are below freezing all year.

Antarctica's seasons are at opposite times to those of the Northern Hemisphere. When the United States is enjoying summer and long hours of daylight, Antarctica is in the middle of its winter and the sun does not shine for three months. In the summer the sun is above the horizon for three months. In between these periods there are varying degrees of twilight. The precipitation that falls is always in the form of snow—an average of 10 inches (25.4 centimeters) per year. Because the area is always under high-pressure air it has a low relative humidity.

Antarctica is somewhat circular in shape. Deep bays cut into its irregular coastline, and on the western side the lengthy Palmer Peninsula juts far out into the Weddell Sea. Actually the whole continent is an island surrounded by the turbulent Antarctic Ocean.

Antarctica is two-thirds as large as North America. The surface of the area is covered by an ice cap, averaging several thousand feet in thickness. Its surface is around 6,000 feet (1,829 meters) above sea level, but at the Pole its altitude is 10,500 feet (3,200 meters). There are mountains underneath the ice, and peaks rise through the ice in some parts. Only one mountain, Mount Erebus, is an active volcano. The interior of Antarctica is an unbroken plateau of ice. It is believed that it would be a solid land mass with many mountains if the ice melted. From time to time the masses of ice and snow slide down, and this movement pushes the border into warmer regions. The ice sometimes melts a little and the ocean tears off huge chunks, known as floes and icebergs. The ice shelves along the coasts are huge masses of ice that extend far out into the water. Some of these rise 30 to 100 feet (9.14—30.48 meters) above the water.

The Ross Ice Shelf, 400 miles (643.7 kilometers) long, is the largest.

One of the strangest features found in Antarctica is the presence of "dry valleys," so called because they are not covered by ice. Since only 5 to 10% of the land is ice-free, these valleys are particularily important because they afford the opportunity to drill directly into the bedrock. The recovery of continuous cores of hard rock and sedimentary rock by the Dry Valley Drilling Project will provide a geological record of Antarctica from the time it was a temperate zone to its present ice-bound condition.

Situated in each of the valleys are glacier-fed lakes and ponds. These bodies of water are regarded by many scientists to be among the most scientifically important in the world. They represent a rare and delicate ecosystem; each one has unique chemical and biological characteristics.

Recently, Antarctica has become known for the large numbers of meteorites recovered on the ice sheets. For example, from 1969 to 1977, over 1,000 meteorites were recovered, representing over one-third of the total amount recovered in the world in the past several centuries.

Little plant life exists in Antarctica. Only a few isolated areas have mosses and lichens. These rare life forms offer the microbiologist clues as to how primitive organisms might exist on other planets, particularly Mars, whose harsh conditions are in many ways similar to those in Antarctica. To marine biologists, the Antarctic waters are the most biologically rich in the world. Cold water sinking to the ocean floor causes the rise of nutrients which provide abundant food for the entire chain of sea life.

There are no living creatures on the land except some tiny insects in summer and a few birds, such as the PENGUIN, ALBATROSS, petrel, and some varieties of gulls.

Antarctica, through the Twelve-Nation Treaty signed in 1959, is to be a scientific preserve. The main objectives of the treaty are to ensure the use of Antarctica for peaceful and scientific purposes, and to continue expeditions started during the International Geophysical Year of 1957-58.

P.P.S./D.E.Z.

SEE ALSO: POLES, NORTH AND SOUTH

**Antares** see Scorpius

**Anteater** True anteaters do not have teeth. They live in tropical America. The giant anteater, about the size of a large dog, lives on the ground. It has coarse hair with a white-edged stripe along its back. The pygmy and lesser anteaters are tree dwellers.

Anteaters eat termites and other small insects. They have long, tube-like noses, like a pig's. A long tongue pops out of the snout to gather in termites. Anteaters also have long, sharp claws to help them uncover termite nests and fight their enemies.

Anteaters are mammals and the babies stay close by the mothers until they are old enough to live in the dense forest by themselves. Some kinds of anteaters live on the ground and have great strength as well as sharp claws to help them survive. Other smaller ones live in trees and have *prehensile* tails, like a monkey's, so that they can swing from branch to branch looking for food. Sticky saliva on the tongue captures the insects after the anteater has broken into a nest. All true anteaters are from Central and South America.

Anteaters, along with sloths and armadillos, are mammals in the order Edentata.

J.C.K.

SEE ALSO: AARDVARK

**Antelope** Antelopes are four-legged hairy mammals. They have split hooves and horns. Many of them look like deer, but they are more closely related to goats, cattle, sheep, and bison. All of these mammals are cud-chewers.

Antelopes vary in size. The Royal Antelope is only 10 inches (25.4 centimeters) high at the shoulder. The Eland weighs 1,200 pounds (544 kilograms). Horns also vary in size and shape. They may be straight, spiraled, or curved. Smaller antelopes may have mere nubbins. Larger ones may have horns 4 feet (1.2 meters) long.

The horns are said to be hollow but actually have a bony core surrounded by hard-ened skin (epidermis). These are true horns and not antlers. Antlers occur in the deer family. They are bony outgrowths not covered by horn and are shed yearly.

Antelopes are ruminant animals. This means they have a four-chambered stomach. All such animals swallow their food without chewing it. Later the food is brought up in small masses to the mouth again and is chewed. The phrase "chewing its cud" refers to the antelope as well as to cattle.

There are no true antelopes native to North America. Most of them are found in Africa. In the western section of North America there is a group of animals who have been named pronghorn antelopes. Though they resemble antelopes, they belong to a different family. Antelopes live in a variety of places. They usually travel in herds or groups. There are many different types of antelopes. Some of the best known varieties include the lesser gnu, the dik-dik, the eland, the impala, the blackbuck, the duikerbok, and the African lechive. Man uses the flesh and the skin of antelopes as he does that of the deer.                    J. C. H.

SEE ALSO: DEER FAMILY

**Blackbuck antelope of India**
Chicago Natural History Museum

**Dik-dik antelope of Abyssinia**
Chicago Natural History Museum

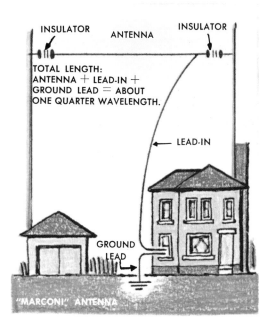

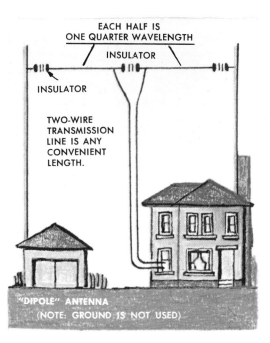

**Antenna (animal)** see Arthropoda

**Antenna (electronic)** An antenna is the portion of a radio system that sends out electrical signals into space or receives these signals from space. The most familiar types of antennas are those found in radio, television, and radar transmitters and receivers.

Radio waves are electromagnetic waves, as are light waves, only much longer. The wavelength of such a wave is the distance it travels through space during the time of one cycle of the AC current in the radiating antenna. It consists of a *magnetic field* and an *electric field*. These steadily exchange energy back and forth between themselves as the wave travels through space.

Electrons, vibrating back and forth in a conductor, set up the original field in the surrounding space and thus launch the wave. As the wave travels through space it passes conducting objects. When it does so, the changing fields in the wave cause the electrons in that conductor to vibrate in step with the wave. This constitutes the AC *signal voltage,* and it operates a radio receiver connected to the conductor. Such a conductor that sends out or receives electromagnetic wave-energy is called an antenna.

A good antenna for producing radio waves should be a metal rod, a wire, or a tower at least one-quarter wavelength long of the operating frequency. Or it should be made electrically this long by adding coils or capacitors. It should be as clear of surrounding trees and buildings as possible.

An antenna made of two rods or wires, each one-quarter wavelength long in one line, is called a *dipole* antenna. It is often used for TV and FM broadcasting and short wave communication. An antenna which is one-quarter wavelength long, or less, and uses the earth as a replacement for the other quarter-wave half is called a *unipole,* or *Marconi* antenna, after the famous pioneer of radio.

It is possible to obtain the length of wire needed to make an antenna. The following formula will give you the length of wire needed in meters.

$$\text{wavelength} = \frac{300}{\text{frequency in megahertz}}$$

C.F.R./A.J.H.

SEE ALSO: BEAM ANTENNA, ELECTRICITY, ELECTRONICS, RADAR, RADIO, TELEVISION

**Anterior** see Animals, classification of

**Anthracite coal** see Coal

**Anthropoid ape** see Ape, Evolution of man, Monkey, Primates

**Anthropology** Anthropology tells about man and how he grew through the ages. It is a long story. It tells about the earliest kinds of people and how they lived. It also tells about the animals they hunted or tamed. Anthropologists may make studies of the habits of different people living on the earth today. An anthropologist is interested in the art, language, family life, biology, and laws of all people since men first came to earth.

The word *anthropology* comes from two Greek words. *Anthropos* means "man," and *logos* means "ordered knowledge." Therefore, anthropology is the ordered knowledge of man. Two main divisions of the knowledge are *cultural anthropology* and *physical anthropology.* According to Ashley Montagu, the noted anthropologist, culture is the man-made part of environment. This includes the pots and pans, the laws, art, religion, and philosophy of man. Therefore, the anthropologist is interested in all forms of social behavior and organized society.

Man's progress may be thought of in a series of three main steps. Step one includes a study of the Lower Paleolithic or early men who lived during the Stone Age and were the last people to make their living mainly through hunting. Step two introduces the first food growers. These were the Neolithic people who can be distinguished as different races. Many of these races found their homes in places now called Europe, Asia, and Africa. In this step was progress in invention and religion, and a higher organization in society. In this stage one could trace the origin of the earliest Americans in the New World, the Indian and his civilization. The third step is the story of man's progress in the development of the "cradles of civilization" in Asia and the early history of Egypt, Crete, and the beginnings of Europe.

Interesting phases of the study of anthropology include the marriage customs, family life, artwork, the making of weapons, and types of written expression of the people of any period. Problems of laws, morality, and religion are also included in a study of anthropology.

Two physical anthropologists, Doctors

Jamaica Tourist Board
**Family life around the world is studied by anthropologists.**

Leakey and Johanson, studied the biology of man, the animal. Their recent digs in Ethiopia and Kenya have uncovered evidence that puts man earlier in the history of civilization than was previously thought. Leakey found skull pieces that existed about 2.5 million years ago. Johanson uncovered numerous bones of a family that he estimated lived a million years before Leakey's ancient creature.

Anthropologists are now beginning to theorize as to which country is the cradle of mankind. Remains uncovered in Europe have caused them to wonder about their long-held theory that earliest man lived in Africa. The years ahead will be exciting ones for young people interested in this ever-changing area of science.    H.J.C.

**Antiaircraft** see Missile

**Antibiotics** Medicines that kill or stop the growth of GERMS which produce disease are called antibiotics. More than sixty different antibiotics are commonly used by medical workers. One of the oldest and best known is PENICILLIN. It is produced by a FUNGUS. Penicillin is used to cure one kind of pneumonia and some kinds of INFECTION that develop when the skin is broken, among other conditions.

Far and Middle Eastern records thousands of years old describe the treatment of skin infections with types of MOLD (small fungus plants) that produce antibiotics. In 1875 LOUIS PASTEUR discovered that when two kinds of BACTERIA come together one type may destroy the other. This is called *antibiosis,* which means life against life.

In 1928, ALEXANDER FLEMING discovered a substance made by a mold that stopped some bacteria from reproducing. He named the substance penicillin. It was later found very effective in treating bacterial pneumonia, streptococcal infections, and VENEREAL DISEASES. Penicillin is effective, inexpensive, and usually safe, but it has drawbacks. It can produce life-threatening allergic reactions. Also, it works against only a few types of bacteria. It is destroyed by stomach acid. Some bacteria produce an ENZYME called *penicillinase* which neutralizes its action. Therefore, a search was made to find other antibiotics that would fight more kinds of infections.

In the 1940s Selman Waksman tested about 10,000 different types of soil bacteria for antibiotic properties. As a result, a new class of antibiotics called *streptomycin* was produced. Unlike penicillin, streptomycin is considered a *broad-spectrum* antibiotic because it is effective against many kinds of bacteria. Other medicines, popularly called antibiotics, are made *synthetically.* Sulfa drugs are examples. The search for new antibiotics continues. *Monobactams,* developed in the 1980s, are effective against diseases that develop in hospitals. By the early 1990s, no safe and effective antibiotics were available for treating certain VIRUS infections, including the common cold and AIDS.

To determine which antibiotic to use to combat treatable infections, a culture is made of the bacteria. Different antibiotics are placed around a culture plate or in a test tube. The most effective antibiotic will prevent the growth of the bacteria. This is called a *sensitivity test.*          B.M.H./E.S.S./J.H.

SEE ALSO: ALLERGY, DRUGS, MEDICINE PHARMACOLOGY, SULFA DRUGS

**Antibody** When GERMS or other unusual substances try to enter the body through the skin or mouth, the body first recognizes that they might be harmful. It usually responds by trying to get rid of them. Antibodies are the substances formed in the blood to defend against the attacking "forces" called *antigens.*

First, both small and large white blood cells are produced in the lymph nodes, bone marrow, spleen, and thymus gland. Some rush to the scene of attack and fight off the attacking germs or BACTERIA. Other white blood cells produce the globulin protein molecules called antibodies. Antibodies specifically "fit" different antigens. They grab and coat the antigen, forming a "complex" that prevents them from spreading. This allows yet another type of white blood cell to actually engulf and destroy the antigen. (This is called phagocytosis.) The remnants of dead cells and antigen-antibody complexes form the pus we see. If the germ itself does not cause a problem, but a poison it produces does, then the poison (called a

| SOME BACTERICIDAL ANTIBIOTICS | SOME INFECTIONS TREATED | SOME BACTERIOSTATIC ANTIBIOTICS | SOME INFECTIONS TREATED |
|---|---|---|---|
| **Penicillins—** | | **Tetracyclines—** | |
| Methicillin, Oxacillin, Cloxacillin, Dicloxacillin | Staphylococcal—venereal disease; rheumatic fever | Achromycin, Terramycin, Declomycin | Plaque, cholera, acne, pneumonia |
| Ampicillin, Amoxycillin | Respiratory, intestinal, urinary | **Chloramphenicol** | Rocky Mountain spotted fever; meningitis; typhoid fever |
| **Streptomycins—** | | | |
| Lincomycin, Clindamycin | Streptococcal, staphylococcal, pneumococcal | **Erythromycin** | Diphtheria; whooping cough; pneumonia; tonsilitis; scarlet fever; Legionnaire's disease |
| Neomycin | Skin, eyes; intestinal tract | | |
| Gentamicin | Bloodstream | | |
| **Cycloserine—Rifampin** | Tuberculosis | **OTHER TYPES ANTIBIOTICS** | **SOME INFECTIONS TREATED** |
| **Cephalosporins** | Skin, bone tissue; urinary tract | **Sulfa—Sulfonamides** | Urinary tract |
| **RECENT VIRAL COMPONENTS** | **SOME INFECTIONS TREATED** | **Antifungal—** | |
| **Antiviral—** | | Nystatin, Amphotercin, Griseofulvin | Fungus; skin, mucous membrane; ringworm |
| Vidarabine | Viral encephalitis | **Protozoa—Paromomycin** | Amebiasis (intestinal tract) |
| Acyclovir (ACV) | Genital herpes | | |
| Azidothymidine (AZT) | AIDS | | |

*toxin)* acts as an antigen (as in botulism). The antibody formed against the toxin can be called an antitoxin.

Most people, once they are exposed to an antigen, form antibodies that will either protect them from or help them fight off other exposures to the same antigen. Some people do not have enough gamma globulin in their blood to protect themselves from infection by forming antibodies. Sometimes they can be given other people's gamma globulin. Protection against disease by having antibodies is called *immunity.*

Some diseases are so severe that people would like to have immunity without actually contracting them. Vaccines have been developed that expose people to small amounts of germs so that they can develop protective antibodies. Examples of successful vaccines include those for smallpox, poliomyelitis (infantile paralysis), and measles. E.S.S.

SEE ALSO: ALLERGY

**Anticyclone** see High pressure center

**Antidote** An antidote is a remedy for poisoning. It may remove the POISON, neutralize it, prevent the body from absorbing it, or assist the body in eliminating it quickly.

**Antifreeze** Antifreeze is any substance which, when added to a liquid, lowers the freezing point of that liquid. It is commonly used in the cooling systems of automobiles, airplanes, tractors, and refrigerators.

Antifreeze is added to the cooling liquid in the radiator of an internal combustion ENGINE. In cold weather it is used alone or with water to prevent the freezing of the cooling system. Also it is used to prevent icing on leading edges of propellers and wings of airplanes.

The most important antifreezes are methanol, ethylene glycol, and ethyl alcohol. Calcium chloride and sodium chloride are used in refrigeration.

Drugs and cosmetics are protected from freezing during storage by means of glycerol and ethyl alcohol. Brand name antifreezes have CORROSION inhibitors added. W. J. K.

SEE ALSO: ALCOHOL

**Antigen** see Allergy, Antibody

**Antihistamine** see Allergy

**Antiknock** see Ethyl

**Antimatter** Antimatter has been discovered in the form of subatomic particles. They are identical to matter particles except they usually have an opposite electrical charge. When matter and antimatter collide, they will destroy each other producing energy.

Positrons (the antiparticles of the electrons), antiprotons, antineutrons and positive pi mesons (the antiparticles of negative pi mesons) have been created by a process known as pair production. High-energy gamma rays or accelerated matter particles are aimed on a heavy atomic nucleus, such as a lead nucleus. Antimatter will be produced in the force field of the nucleus. For example, a gamma ray will change into an electron and a positron. An accelerated proton will change into a new proton and an antiproton.

Since our planet is made of matter, there is a great probability that the antiparticles will soon react with a matter particle and change back into energy. This is the reason that antimatter is seldom found on earth.

Scientists theorize that if there were no matter, entire atoms could be made of antiparticles. This might be possible in outer space. Some stars may be made entirely of antimatter. B. A. T.

SEE ALSO: ATOM, MATTER, NUCLEAR SCIENCE

**Antimony** (ANT-ih-moh-nee) Antimony is a shiny, gray, solid chemical element that looks much like lead. Chemists find that it behaves both as a metal and as a nonmetal. It combines with oxygen or with sulfur as would a metal; yet with sodium or lithium, as would a nonmetal. Unlike most metals, it is brittle and conducts electricity poorly.

Antimony sulfide was known (stibnite) in ancient times. Ladies then used it as eye makeup calling it *kohl.* Most compounds of antimony are poisonous.

Antimony increases in volume as it changes from a hot liquid into a cooled solid. For this reason it is added to printer's type metal and to the plates of automobile batteries, making them harder and sharper in outline. Antimony is used in some electronic devices. Many ALLOYS contain antimony. Antimony sesquisulfide, $Sb_2S_3$, is widely used as the fuel component of matches.

The chemical symbol of antimony is Sb; its atomic number is 51; its atomic mass, 121.75. It is in Group IV of the Periodic Table. It is refined from stibnite.    C. F. R.
SEE ALSO: ATOM, ELEMENTS

**Antineutron** see Antimatter

**Antiparticle** see Antimatter

**Antiproton** see Antimatter

**Antiseptic** An antiseptic is a substance which either destroys germs that cause disease or prevents them from multiplying. Antiseptics are usually man-made chemical solutions. However, the *ultraviolet light* from the sun is an excellent *disinfectant*. There are many antiseptic solutions made to help prevent infections of wounds in the skin.

A distinction must be made between antisepsis and STERILIZATION. In the process of antisepsis, one hopes to kill off disease germs, or at least to prevent them from reproducing too fast. In sterilization temperature is raised so high that it kills all disease-producing germs. The instrument that has been sterilized will then be said to be aseptic—meaning germ free.

Beginning in 1850, LOUIS PASTEUR investigated the process of fermentation and decay of organic material. He was the first to discover that decay and certain diseases are caused by living organisms, very often bacteria. A British doctor, JOSEPH LISTER, heard of these experiments and attempted to sterilize his surgery by using antiseptics. He sprayed *carbolic acid* around the operating rooms and hospital wards before performing surgery or dressing wounds. There was a great deal of opposition to Dr. Lister's theories among medical men of those times, but he was eventually proven to be correct in his attack

✳ **THINGS TO DO**

**DO ANTISEPTICS DESTROY GERMS?**

1   Make a bacteria culture by contaminating agar which has been prepared (see BACTERIOLOGY) in sterilized petri dishes. Let the bacteria grow for several days in a warm dark place.
2   Take a piece of cotton which has been soaked in alcohol (an antiseptic) and rub it across part of the bacteria culture. What happened to the whitish patches, bacteria colonies, that were touched by the antiseptic?

upon bacteria. Thus began the era of modern surgery.

Modern surgery is conducted aseptically. The patient, operating room, personnel, and instruments are all made as germ free as possible before surgery is begun. In addition, antiseptics are still used on the skin.

The effectiveness of an antiseptic depends upon its concentration, the duration of its contact with a surface it can penetrate, and the temperature. In general, an antiseptic is more effective at warmer temperatures.

Chlorine is an effective antiseptic for use in swimming pools and in drinking water, where it prevents the multiplication of disease-producing bacteria, particularly the organism that causes TYPHOID FEVER. Other important antiseptics are iodine, hydrogen peroxide, mercury in solution, detergents, soaps, and ethyl alcohol.    B. M. H.
SEE ALSO: ALCOHOL, INFECTION

**Antitoxin** see Antibody, Vaccine

**Antler** see Deer family, Horn

**Ants** Ants are small insects with six legs. Like BEES, they are social insects. They dig tunnels in the ground or in wood where they make their homes and store food. A great many of them share the same home, food, and care of ant eggs and ant larvae. A large group of ants living and working together is called a *colony*.

Most authorities believe that the ants form a very large group in the insect world. They estimate that there are between two and five thousand species in existence. They also find that all these different species are very much alike in their structure and their habits.

An ant body is divided into three parts—head, thorax, and abdomen.

The head is connected to the thorax (mid body) by a narrow "neck." The thorax is joined to the abdomen by a short "waist."

On the head of an ant are feelers (antennae). Next to the head, a feeler has one long section followed by a number of beadlike sections. At the tip, the feeler is thicker because it has many sense organs. On one of them there may be 200 or more olfactory cones for smelling and 1,000 or more hairs sensitive to touch. Feelers are almost always moving in order to smell and feel in all directions.

Also on the head are compound eyes, made of many small eyes and mouthparts. The jaws (mandibles) are large and used for carrying, digging, grasping, and tearing. Other mouthparts taste food, clean antennae, and

✳ **THINGS TO DO**

**CONSTRUCTING AND STOCKING AN ANT COLONY**

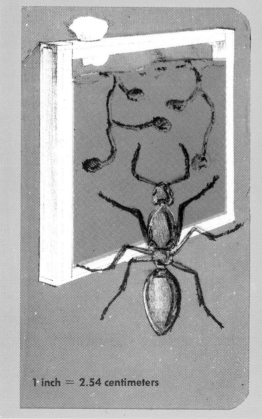

1 inch = 2.54 centimeters

**Materials: two sheets of 12″ by 18″ glass, two wooden strips 1″ by 1″ by 12″, two strips 16″, dark paper**

1 Build the ant home according to the illustration. Drill a hole in the top piece of wood through which food and water may be put. A cotton plug in the hole will keep ants inside. Keep the top piece moveable for stocking the colony. Tape the other edges.

2 Locate an ant hill. Dig up one square foot of soil around it. Place the soil and ants on a piece of white cloth. Examine the contents until the queen is located. The workers will not live without the female in the colony. Transfer the colony to the new home. A newspaper funnel may be used to get the ants and soil from the cloth into the narrow structure.

3 Cover the glass with dark paper for two weeks to encourage the ants to make tunnels and rooms close to the sides for observation. Ants need honey, sugar water, and wet sponge placed on top of the soil line.

chew. A "tongue" on the lower "lip" (labium) cleans and takes in foods.

On the thorax are three pairs of jointed legs. The abdomen is rounded and segmented. Inside are the digestive organs.

Ants are social insects, living together in large communities. Individual ants take in food to feed the group. When the first stomach or crop is full, part of the food is vomited up and given to the queen and larvae. Some of the food passes to a second stomach where it is digested and used by the individual.

The most important ant in a colony is the queen. She lays all of the eggs. Her ovaries, in the abdomen, are very large and she may lay eggs every few minutes.

Most of the other ants in the colony are workers. They are all females, but their sex organs are underdeveloped. Thus they cannot lay eggs. These ants care for the queen, for the eggs laid by the queen, and for the larvae hatching from the eggs. When the larvae become pupae they too are cared for by workers. Workers also gather the food that is shared and build and repair the nest. Among some ants there are two kinds of workers. Small ones stay in the nest and larger ones occupy themselves with outside work.

Soldier ants have very large heads and jaws. They guard the colony but are not as aggressive as the workers, who usually kill the prey. Soldiers, with their powerful jaws, tear the victim into small enough pieces for the workers to carry. Soldiers are also underdeveloped females.

At certain times males appear in the colony. They are winged, living long enough to fertilize a few young females. Young females are winged and leave the nest to establish new colonies. They are accompanied on their flight by the males. A female receives enough sperm to last for the rest of her life. Males die immediately after the "marriage flight." Those males who did not fertilize a female starve to death.

After the flight, the female breaks off her wings by scraping them against stones on the ground. When the wings are off, the female is called a queen. She searches for a place to build a nest. Some ants select rotten wood, others dig in the ground or nest under stones. After selecting the site, the queen seals herself off in a cell and begins to lay eggs. The first workers appear one to nine months later

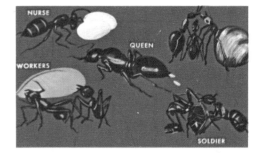

**Ants live in large groups. Each kind, or caste, of ant has its own work to do**

depending upon the species of ant. During this period, the queen obtains nourishment from her thoracic wing muscles and from a certain percentage of the eggs she lays. To hasten pupation, she gives the largest larvae most of the food. In one species, the queen kills the workers in another colony and carries off the pupae. By this action she shortens the waiting period for workers and staves off starvation. When the first workers appear, they enlarge the nest and begin caring for eggs and larvae.

Ants feed upon plants, animals, or both. Thus they may be herbivorous, carnivorous, or omnivorous.                          J. C. K.
SEE ALSO: INSECTA

**Anus**  see Digestive system

**Anvil**  see Ear

**Aorta**  see Artery, Circulatory system

**Apatite**  (AP-uh-tyte)  The mineral apatite is composed mainly of calcium phosphate. However, small amounts of calcium fluoride or calcium chloride may be present. The name comes from the Greek *apate* which means "deception." The mineral is well named since it does resemble several other minerals.

Apatite is always found in bones and teeth. Commercially this mineral is used to make fertilizer and phosphoric acid. Apatite may occur in a variety of colors. It has a white streak, glassy luster, hardness of 5, and a specific gravity of 3.1. It is found in rocks of all classes where it occurs as small crystals. Extensive "pebble" phosphate deposits in Florida supply most of the United States' needs. Other large deposits are found in North Africa.        S.G./P.P.S.

SEE ALSO: ROCKS

Gibbon

Chicago Natural History Museum

Orangutan

**Ape** Of all the animals, apes are most nearly like man. The brain, the nervous system, and the blood of apes are all quite similar to man's. The CHIMPANZEE, the ORANGUTAN, the GORILLA and the GIBBON are four groups of animals which may be called apes.

The bodies of apes usually have brown, reddish-brown, or black hair except on faces, feet, and hands. Both feet can be used like hands since both hands and feet have "thumbs" to help them grasp and handle objects. Apes do not have tails.

Though these four animals have a general physical resemblance to each other, they are in some ways different from each other. Some apes use all four limbs in walking, and others walk mainly on their hind legs. When

Chimpanzee

Courtesy Society For Visual Education, Inc.

Gorilla

A comparison of the skeletons of man and ape reveals why man stands erect while his close relative, the ape, does not. The bones at the back of the neck on the ape keep its head thrust forward and down

full grown there is a great difference in the heights and weights of the four groups of apes. The gibbon seldom measures more than 3 feet (.9 meters), whereas the gorilla frequently grows to a height of nearly 6 feet (1.8 meters). Gorillas have been known to weigh over 400 pounds (181.4 kilograms) when full grown.

Apes can climb very easily. In their natural state most of them live in trees. That is why they are *arboreal,* meaning "tree-dwellers." Some apes build nests in the branches of trees. These nests are usually made of leaves, twigs, and small branches. Apes prefer fruits and vegetables for food although they also eat eggs, small animals, nuts, and insects. Apes can be found in Southeast Asia, the East Indies, Borneo, Sumatra, Central and West Africa.

Apes are gregarious animals, dwelling in family groups rather than alone. They are referred to as *anthropoids,* meaning "like man" or "resembling man."     G.A.D.

SEE ALSO: MONKEY, PRIMATES, SKELETON

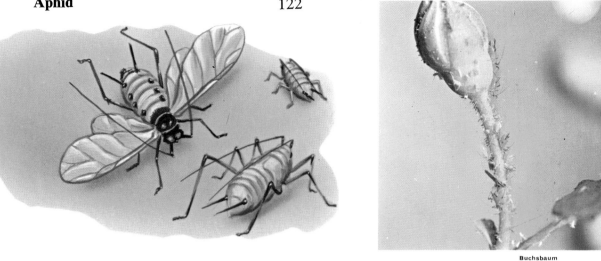

Buchsbaum

**Rose growers are familiar with the damage the tiny aphids can do to the delicate rose plants**

**Aphid** The aphid is a small insect which attacks plants. It sucks juices from the tender cells of plant parts. Such plants as corn, oats, wheat, roses, and other bushes, plus vines and fruit trees are its common sources of food.

It has a plump body and a small head with a sharp, sucking beak. A few aphids have wings but most of them, including females, are wingless. Green, black or white are their usual colors. For protection it spreads a white, wavy secretion over its body.

While the aphid eats, it exudes sweet droplets called "honeydew" through the anus, located near the tip of its abdomen. ANTS in particular are extremely fond of this liquid and sometimes maintain whole colonies of aphids to be assured of a supply of it. If this honeydew is not gathered by ants, it appears as dew on the plant leaves. Occasionally bees will gather it when there is little pollen, but because it thins and sours quickly, an inferior honey is made from it.

An aphid does not live long, but so many generations are born in just one summer that this insect's chances of dying out are slim. The mating time is in the fall when the eggs are placed in protected parts of plants, such as between layers of bark of trees. The following spring the eggs hatch. These aphids are all females and within three to four days produce other aphids from eggs within their bodies. All during the feeding season succeeding generations are born. In the fall the last groups include males.

The destructive force of these insects is extremely great. The leaves of plants will curl up or drop off; GALL-like swellings will appear on the roots and bark whenever an aphid inhabits a plant. Fortunately, the insect has many enemies: the spider and the lady-bird beetle plus the lacewing fly, syrphus fly, and the greatest of all enemies, the chalcid fly, which is itself a parasite. Beside these are the sprays which are effective in controlling the aphid.           D.E.Z.

SEE ALSO: INSECTA

**Apiculture** see Bees

**Apogee** The orbit of any natural or man-made SATELLITE is never perfectly circular, nor is the Earth exactly at the center of the ORBIT. The point in the revolution of a satellite at which it is farthest from Earth is called the *apogee*.

SEE: PERIGEE

**Apoplexy** Apoplexy is the condition in which one loses consciousness, sensation, or ability to move because a blood vessel in the brain has broken or become stopped up. It is also called a stroke or CVA (Cerebro Vascular Accident).

SEE ALSO: THROMBOSIS

**Appalachian Mts.** see North America

**Appendix** The appendix is a finger-like sac attached near the beginning of the large intestine. It is located in the lower right hand side of the ABDOMEN. The portion of the large intestine below its connection with the small intestine is called the *cecum*. There is an opening in the cecum which ends in an extension—the appendix. It may be from 1 to 6 inches (2.54-15.24 centimeters) in length. As far as is known, the appendix serves no useful function in the human body, but is a remainder of a useful cecum in ancestral forms.

Inflammation of the appendix *(appendicitis)* may cause severe and sometimes fatal illness. INFLAMMATION may result from infection within the appendix and may arise when bacteria collect and multiply. Infection in the appendix usually results in swelling, which often makes it impossible for the materials inside to be emptied. Continued swelling, complicated by trapped toxic materials, may cause the appendix to burst. The spread of the infection to the lining of the abdominal walls causes *peritonitis.* This can be fatal. Inflammation of the appendix may also be caused by the lodging of foreign bodies within the appendix. Surgery to remove the inflamed appendix is almost always curative.       G.A.D.

SEE ALSO: DIGESTIVE SYSTEM

**The appendix is a small sac attached to the large intestine**

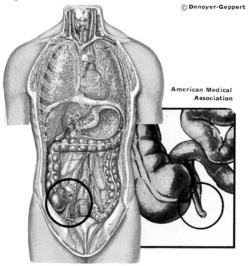

© Denoyer-Geppert

American Medical Association

Apple tree and fruit

**Apple** Apples are a valuable fruit. They can be grown almost anywhere in the world, and they provide important minerals and vitamins for the human diet.

When the first settlers came to America, they brought apple trees with them to plant in the new world. Today the United States grows more apples than any other country.

The apple is in genus *Malus* of the rose family. The tree grows to about 40 feet (12.2 meters). The fragrant pink and white apple blossoms appear late in spring. The flower has three circles of stamens and five carpels in the ovary. When fertilized, it develops into an *accessory fruit.* The endocarp is paper-like and contains the seeds. The rest of the fruit wall is fleshy and makes up the major portion of the edible fruit. Most apple trees are grown by *budding,* grafting the buds of one plant into the bark near the roots of another.

Over 80% of apple tissue is water and sugar. It possesses very little protein and even less fat. During the ripening process, the starch molecules are changed to sugar, and the amount of malic acid, which gives the sour taste, is reduced. The mealiness of apples occurs when the *parenchyma* cells become soft. By using yeast, apple juice can be changed to cider and then to vinegar.       H. J. C.

SEE ALSO: FRUIT, PROPAGATION

**Apricot** This is the name for a small tree and the fruit it produces. The tree grows between 20 and 30 feet (6.1-9.1 meters) high. The pink flowers bloom just before the leaves come. The fruit is fleshy with a hard pit surrounding the single seed. The skin of the fruit is not furry as on the peach. Apricots are called stone fruits.                    P.G.B.

**Aquaculture** Farming in water instead of on land is called aquaculture. Both plants and animals can be raised under a somewhat controlled environment Shellfish and lobsters can be grown to adulthood in a tank of salt water. Fish and many MOLLUSKS are kept in cages under water. Algae and other water plants can be produced in abundance.

Aquaculture is a fast-growing science. As man uses up land areas, he looks to the water for farming crops. Caged aquatic animals, when fed routinely, offer great advantages. Man can control the time of maturity, and every creature can be caught. An acre (.4047 hectares) will yield over 5,000 pounds (2,268 kilograms) of fish. However, there are problems related to aquaculture. Feeding the animals means raising aquatic plants, their normal diet. It is more difficult to fertilize algae, for currents carry the nutrients out to sea. Even though

Fish can be raised as a crop.

*Glen Smart; National Fish and Wildlife Service*

algae are more efficient users of the sun's energy than land plants, they do not produce well in direct sunlight or growing conditions become too crowded.

Farming the coastal areas is producing another environmental problem. It is interrupting the breeding grounds of many of the ocean's game fish. Eggs are laid, and the young live in these waters for a while.

An unexpected advantage of nuclear power plants is the use of the ponds or lagoons which receive warm water from their cooling systems. Fish raised here have been producing a crop of 200,000 pounds (90,718.4 kilograms) annually. The science of salmon and algae farming is becoming as technical as that for cows and wheat.     H.J.C.

SEE ALSO: AGRICULTURE

*Metaframe Corporation Living World*

**Aquarium** An aquarium is a glass house for plants and animals that live in water. This glass house may be a large jar or a round bowl. It may have flat glass sides with metal edges and a glass top. About 2 inches (5.08 centimeters) of well-washed sand or gravel is placed on the bottom of the aquarium. Marbles or clean rocks can also be used. Water plants are needed in the aquarium. They not only are decoration but they give food and oxygen to the other living things in the water. An aquarium may also mean a building in which tanks of fresh or salt water animals are kept.

There are two large groups of water ani-

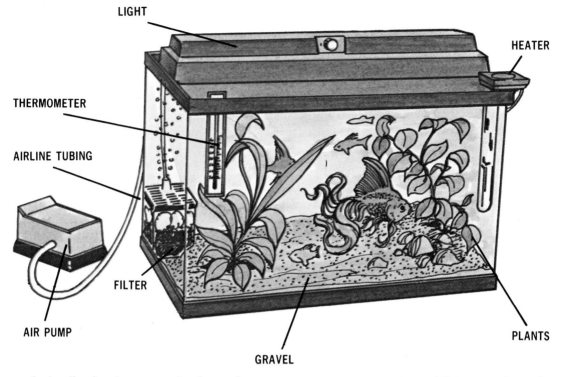

mals that live in a home or school aquarium. One group is called "cold water" animals. They are goldfish, tadpoles, minnows, and water insects found in streams and lakes. The water temperature for this group should be kept between 55° and 72° F. (12.8° to 22.2° C.). The other group is made up of "warm water" animals, including all tropical fish. Some of these are guppies, platys, tetras, zebras, swordtails, mallies, and angel fish. These fish like their water temperature between 72° and 80° F. (22.2° to 26.7° C.).

Some aquatic plants survive well when submerged in water. The most common are the ribbon-like grasses, Vallisneria and Sagittaria. These may be used in either cold or warm water tanks. Other desirable water plants are Hygraphia, Ludwiga, Elodea, and Cabomba. These plants must be weighted down with lead ribbons or stones to remain in a stationary and vertical position. Floating plants such as the Salvinia (fern) or Lemna (duckweed) are also used. Goldfish especially like to feed on Lemna. Plants furnish the oxygen needed by the fish and in turn use the carbon dioxide given off by the fish as a raw material for PHOTOSYNTHESIS. Plants also serve as hiding places for baby fish.

Cold water animals need more space and surface area than tropical fish. A general rule is to keep an inch of fish to a gallon of water (2.54 centimeters of fish to 3.78 liters of water). This margin of safety may be reduced if mechanical aeration is used.

The water for an aquarium should be free of chlorine and other chemicals added in water filtration. Allowing the water to stand for 2 days will let these chemicals dissipate. In some areas the water should be checked to see what amounts of acid or alkali are present. A special water softener of baking soda (½ teaspoon to 10 gallons or 37.85 liters of water) may be used for overly acid water. After this settling period, the fish may be added. A few snails can act as scavengers in keeping the aquarium clear.

Temperature is an important factor to a plant and animal life tank. The larger the tank, the less rapid is the cooling of water, especially if thermostatically controlled heaters are not used, and room temperature changes radically within a 24 hour period.

M.E.C.

SEE ALSO: PLANTS, AQUARIUM; TROPICAL FISH

**Aquarius** see Water Bearer

**Aquatic life** see Marine biology

**Aqueduct** see Bridges, Irrigation

**Aqueous humor** see Eye

Aquila is "The Eagle"

**Aquila** (AK-wi-luh) The name Aquila means "eagle." The people of long ago who named this CONSTELLATION felt that its stars formed a picture of an eagle. Aquila cannot be seen in the Northern Hemisphere in the winter. It can only be viewed from spring to autumn and is classed as a summer constellation.

The four main stars of this constellation form the shape of a T. If modern astronomers were naming this constellation, they probably would call it an airplane. But many years ago it was compared to an eagle by the people of several different nations. The Hebrews, the Greeks, the Romans, and the Arabs all thought it looked like an eagle.

*Altair,* the brightest star in the constellation, is at the cross-point. It is one of the twenty brightest stars in the sky. With two other very bright stars, Vega and Deneb, Altair forms a large triangle known as the Summer Triangle.

Altair is a bluish star and it has a smaller star on each side of it. This line of three stars makes the Eagle a fairly easy constellation to find in the summer.　　　　　c. l. k.

**Arachnida** (uh-RAK-nid-uh) Arachnids are a class of animals. Their bodies are made up of two parts and they have four pairs of jointed legs. Spiders, mites, ticks and scorpions belong to the arachnid class. They are different from insects because they have no wings, feelers (antennae), or mandibles for chewing.

They may have claws, poison glands, or stingers. The SPIDER can secrete a

fluid from which it spins a web. Contact with air hardens the fluid.

The most common homes of arachnids are in warm, dry regions, but some varieties may be found in almost all climates. Some live in water.

Most arachnids are harmless creatures. Some help man by destroying harmful insects. Other varieties are damaging to animals and plants. These include the black widow spider, whose bite can be harmful to man. SCORPION stings are also painful. Some kinds of TICKS and MITES are disease carriers. Other mites do damage to plants by sucking their juices.

The arachnid's body has an outer skeleton—*exoskeleton*—on the abdomen and on the combined head and thorax. The exoskeleton is made up of chitinous tissue which serves as an attachment for the complex muscular system.

Internal body structure of arachnids follows the general pattern of other animals. The digestive system is made up of three parts which resemble intestines of other animals. The circulatory system includes a tubular heart. Some varieties breathe by means of tracheal tubes. Other have one or more pairs of *book lungs* (parallel air pockets) which receive air from a slit in the body wall.

Arachnids have a brain and central nervous system. Touch is their most highly developed sense. Sensory hairs for touch may be found on all parts of the body. Arachnids have simple rather than compound eyes. Scorpions have as many as ten pairs of eyes.

The sense of smell is poorly developed. Hearing ability has not been determined. However, some arachnids have sound-making devices. This would indicate that they are able to hear.

**The garden spider is a common arachnid**
Courtesy Society For Visual Education, Inc.

KEEPING ARACHNIDS AS PETS

Materials: two cake pans, fine wire mesh, plaster of Paris, branching sticks

1   Construct a cage by putting a cylinder of fine wire mesh upright in a cake pan of wet plaster of Paris. Allow it to harden. Use the other cake pan as a removeable cover. Insert several sticks for spiders to attach their webs.

2   In the grass of open fields and under logs or rocks, many species of arachnids may be found. Capture them in a jar to transport back to their new home. In the fall the egg cases of spiders may also be collected.

3   Arachnids need water daily but may go for weeks without food. Keep a wet sponge in the cage and occasionally drop in live, soft-bodied insects or meal-worms for food.

4   Arachnids are fascinating animals to observe. They will live and reproduce in captivity.

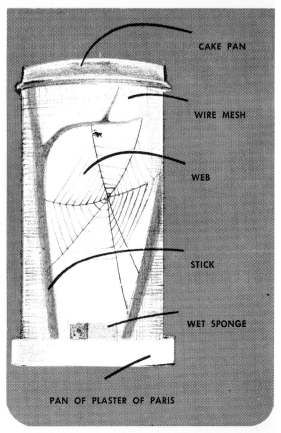

CAKE PAN

WIRE MESH

WEB

STICK

WET SPONGE

PAN OF PLASTER OF PARIS

Reproduction of arachnids is by means of eggs. The female arachnid lays a great many eggs at once. Some varieties, including spiders, form an egg sac to protect their young until after they are hatched.

Arachnids have been classed by scientists into sixteen different orders, five of which are extinct. The name "arachnid" is from a Greek word *arachne* which means "spider."

I. H. S.

SEE ALSO: ARTHROPODA

**Arboretum**   An arboretum is a garden of trees and shrubs. It is divided into sections for different families of trees and other plants. Flowering trees may be in one section, nut groves in another, and evergreens in still another. The purposes of such a garden are to give scientists a place to try out new ideas and to give nature lovers a place where they can see a great many varieties of trees and shrubs at once.

The idea of arboretums is not new. As far back as 2800 B.C. arboretums flourished in some Eastern countries. However, it was not until the middle of the eighteenth century that influential men gave money for the development of such gardens. Some of these were in France, London, England, and Japan. The first arboretum in the United States was the Linnaean Botanical Garden started in 1793, and its influence on future arboretums was very great. In America, three of the most famous ones today are the Arnold Arboretum in Boston, Massachusetts; the Morton Arboretum in Downers Grove, Illinois; and the National Arboretum in Washington, D.C.

All arboretums are not alike. Some have a representation of all the trees and shrubs common to that region. Others have only certain types of trees. Most arboretums are arranged so that all the members of one plant family grow in one section and those of another species grow in the next section. New and rare plants are also raised, and various experiments are made with different kinds of soil. In one respect all arboretums are alike, for they pass on the information they have learned to other arboretums and to scientists.

The values of such a garden are many. They include growing a complete collection of one set of plants, testing and introducing new plants, providing a laboratory for botanists, helping schools, conserving the plant life of the region, training gardeners, and giving information to other institutions and agencies.                         D. E. Z.

SEE ALSO: HORTICULTURE

The arborvitae is a conifer of the north

**Arborvitae** (AHR-ber-VY-tee)   Arborvitae is the name given to some kinds of cone-bearing trees and shrubs belonging to the cypress and cedar family. They have flat branches with small overlapping leaves. RESIN glands similar to oil glands of the skin are located on the leaves. The twigs are covered with tiny scales. Cones are always small.

Arborvitae resemble CYPRESS trees. They grow mainly in north temperate regions. The northern white CEDAR, a variety of arborvitae found in the New England and lake states, does not grow to a large size. The western red cedar, in contrast, is a giant arborvitae. Its native habitat is the forests of Washington and Oregon.

The wood of arborvitae is light, soft, and fragrant. It is resistant to decay and is used for the manufacture of shingles and fence posts. The giant arborvitae is used in the construction of boat hulls. The fibers of the bark are used for weaving mats and baskets.                         I. H. S.

**Arc**   When an electrical current flows from one ELECTRODE to another electrode by jumping across an air gap, an *arc* is created in that small air space. The electrode may be a wire or any material which can carry a current.

Three common properties of electric arcs are: 1) they reach very high temperatures (thousands of degrees centigrade in some applications); 2) they concentrate a high heat energy; 3) they usually produce a brilliant light. Electric arcs have applications where extremes of heat and light are required.

Arc furnaces are used in foundries and steel mills to melt metal. The arc furnace is employed for melting smaller batches than other type furnaces normally melt. The electrical current is passed from an electrode through an arc to the metal being melted. The metal acts as the other electrode and completes the electrical circuit.

Arc lamps, or *carbon arc lamps* as they are normally called, usually consist of two pure carbon electrodes which, when properly adjusted, give off an intensely bright light. Sometimes the arc is in a gas or vapor which also becomes illuminated and adds still further to the brightness. Carbon electrodes have a very high resistance to current flow, but once the current does start by touching the electrodes together, the resistance decreases rapidly. Current limiting controls must be provided for carbon arc applications. As light is produced from the arc, the carbon electrodes are slowly burned away. In order to maintain maximum brightness, the width of the gap must be adjusted constantly, either by hand or by an automatic device. Lamps of this type are used in movie projectors, searchlights and blueprint machines.

An electric arc produces very high temperatures useful in welding

Arc welding is a welding process where the highly concentrated heat of the electric arc is used to melt and join metals. Electric arc welding can be accomplished by four different methods:

1) *Carbon electrode arc*—two carbon electrodes at a slight angle to one another provide an arc to melt the joint. A filler metal can be added. 2) *Metal arc*—the most common form of welding consists of a metal rod used as one electrode, and the metal to be welded serving as the other. The rod is covered with a special coating to prevent slag from forming. 3) *Submerged metal arc*—the arc is buried in a mound of granular fusible material. This is used for large, heavy welds. 4) *Inert gas-metal arc*—a stream of inert gas (argon or helium) surrounds the metal arc to shield against the formation of impurities and spatter. This is a fast, high-quality weld.          E. I. D.

## Archaeopteryx (ark-ee-OPP-tuh-ricks)
These birds lived in the Jurasic period, about 135-181 million years ago. They are the oldest known birds. They resemble both reptiles and birds.

Remains of Archaeopteryx, which means "ancient wing," were discovered in limestone caves in Solenhofen, Germany. The body was about the size of a large crow. Its reptilian characteristics were three-clawed fingers on each wing, bony teeth set in sockets, and a long tail. It was birdlike in having wings with true feathers, slender four-toed legs, and a skull somewhat like that of a modern bird. The jaw was drawn out into a beak and its eyes were large.          J. C. K.

SEE ALSO: GEOLOGIC TIME TABLE

**Reconsrruction of an archaeopteryx**

Indian relics found in the Southwest show facts about tribal cultures of long ago. Archeologists can reconstruct customs from such finds

**Archeology** (ark-ee-OHL-oh-gee) Archeology is the study of ancient times by means of the tools and other objects left behind by early man. The archeologist searches for man-made objects (*artifacts*), such as arrowheads and pottery jars, and tries to figure out how and when they were used. In the Americas archeologists study the culture of Indians who lived before the arrival of Columbus. In other parts of the world they search for buried cities or caves and campfires of the first men on earth.

Spear heads, axes, knives, scrapers, jars, ornaments, household utensils, furniture,

Dickson Mounds

Archeologists often use artifacts to reconstruct the past. (Above) A museum reconstruction of an Indian living quarters. (Right) Young archeologists carefully search for relics of the past.

Field Museum of Natural History

foundations of houses, temples, ruins of a village burying ground, carvings on cave walls, and the bones and shells around a campfire can tell something about the people who made and used them. Some of these are found accidentally when people plow fields, build roads, or dig pits. Other discoveries are based on careful exploration.

Artifacts are best preserved in desert sand, in dry cold, in continuously frozen soil, and in peat bogs. Dry sand has preserved for more than 4,000 years all the treasures, even linen cloth, in the Egyptian tombs. (Meat of the extinct mammoth found in the ice was edible after more than 10,000 years of refrigeration.)

It is the task of the archeologist to supervise the careful excavation of these finds. Sand and soil, in many cases, must be removed gently, by hand, so that none of the objects will be disturbed and so that their exact positions may be recorded. The second step—accurately cataloging, describing, illustrating, and photographing—is a most important one. These are the clues needed to make comparisons and to reconstruct the history of the men who lived so long ago. Many objects need special treatment to preserve them. Archeologists also have been engaged in the restoration of ancient temples and palaces.

In the 19th century, excavations of Pompeii and Herculaneum in Italy uncovered these cities that had been buried for seventeen hundred years after the eruption of Mount Vesuvius in 79 A.D.

Some of the work done after the finding of Pompeii has laid a firm foundation for modern archeological studies. An Englishman, Flinders Petrie, and an American, James Breasted, were among the many who uncovered the ancient tombs and temples of Egypt. The deciphering of the Rosetta Stone by Jean-Francois Champollion gave scholars the key to hieroglyphic inscription—the writing of long-lost languages. E.H. Thompson discovered the sacred well of a Mayan city in the jungles of Yucatan. Heinrich Schliemann found nine cities of Troy, each one built above the ruins of another.

One of the most sensational finds in the history of archeology took place on November 26, 1922. After years of searching for the tomb of the Egyptian pharoah, Tutankhamun, archeologist Howard Carter,

Aerial view of an archeological dig.

Del Baston

Egyptian Government Tourist Office

**The tomb of Ramses II is in the Valley of the Kings. When Egypt built the Aswan High Dam it was necessary to move this more than 3,000-year-old tomb to avoid the rising waters of the Nile River.**

Lord Carnarvon, and a few companions stood at the entrance of his newly discovered tomb in Egypt's Valley of the Kings. Inside the tomb, placed in a solid gold coffin, lay the remains of the young king. Surrounding it were almost incredible riches.

Prior to this discovery, only scattered remnants of the treasures of other pharoahs had come to light. Grave robbing in ancient Egypt was a common practice. Every other royal tomb had been looted of its treasures. In most cases, the robbers entered the tombs almost immediately after burial. Such was the case with Tutankhamun's tomb, but apparently the robbers were caught and the tomb resealed. The treasures left with the pharoah were designed to comfort and delight his spirit in the journey to the afterlife. The objects reflect a high degree of craftsmanship from one of the most important periods of Egyptian art. By studying these artifacts, archeologists can gain a better understanding of what life was like in ancient Egypt over 3,000 years ago.

There are many ways to determine the age of artifacts. The nine cities of Troy illustrate the principle of super-position. Those on top are the youngest, or newest, and the lower layers are the oldest. Rocks are found in layers, or strata, and annual layers of pebbles and sediment are deposited in lakes. By this system of *stratigraphy,* man-made objects are dated according to the layers in which they are found.

Finding bones of animals known to have existed only during the Ice Ages helped determine when the Folsom and Sandia weapons were used.

Dr. Willard Libby discovered it was possible to determine how long ago bits of charcoal or bone had been burned in a campfire by measuring the amount of carbon-14

($C^{14}$) still remaining in the samples. A mammoth tusk from Sandia Cave dates back 26,000 years. This $C^{14}$ process dates some corn taken from the cave to be about 5,000 years old.

Chemists also use atomic-age instruments to help them date artifacts. Infrared spectrometry is used to study amber and copper deposits. Thermoluminescence is a method of determining the rate of uranium and thorium decay. During the decay process some electrons get trapped in the object. By applying heat and measuring the light given off when these electrons escape, the chemist can determine the age of a clay artifact. One drawback to this technique is that some clays have a higher concentration to begin with and this must be determined in order for the dating to be accurate. Other methods employ X-ray fluorescence and neutron-activation analysis.

Now that chemists are more interested in and experimenting with archeology a whole new field of analyses has developed. These analyses are referred to as "chemical fingerprinting" of metals. Artifacts can be examined and classified according to their impurities and geographical location. This helps archeologists to plot the migration of early people and the location of specific natural resources.

Archeological expeditions are organized and financed by governments, museums, universities, and foundations. Very often these archeological "digs" employ volunteers to aid in the recovery of artifacts. When the construction of dams or highways threatens an area rich in ancient artifacts, archeologists will work with the construction workers to preserve as much as possible of the remains. In Rome, when municipal construction uncovers ruins, work will stop until the site can be studied. Unfortunately, in some ancient cities such care is not being taken, and the ancient ruins are being destroyed. P.P.S./A.P.M.

SEE ALSO: PALEONTOLOGY, STONE AGE

**A cut-away of the Hopewell Indian burial mound from 100 A.D. shows levels of buried artifacts**

Chicago Natural History Museum

**Archeozoic Era** (ahr-kee-uh-ZOH-ick) Archeozoic Era is the name given to the period in the earth's history to which the oldest rocks belong. It is thought that some form of plant life was present at that time.

The lava rocks and sediments from the Archeozoic Era, dating from two to one billion years ago, are found all over the world—in Canada, northern Europe, Australia, Africa, and in North and South America. Dating from radioactive minerals has shown rocks of this age to be at the base of or eroded on the surface of the Adirondacks, Colorado Rocky Mountains and Black Hills, and in the Grand Canyon. The presence of gold and silver has increased the search for Archaean (the very oldest) rock.

No fossils have been found in these rocks, but some formations in the limestone are believed to be evidence of some kind of sea plant. The presence of graphite, or lead, has been suggested as another clue to the existence of plant life in this era.

Geologists distinguish two kinds of ancient rock formations—the upper sedimentary Timiskaming rocks, and the lower, or Keewatin, greenstone rocks. The lower rocks sometimes have a peculiar "pillow" shape caused by lava dropping into water. These are deformed and changed (metamorphosed) so that the original composition is not known. Granites, gneisses and schists are found in this group.

During this era, the oldest mountains in North America, the Laurentians in Canada, were formed.

The Archeozoic Era is followed by the PROTEROZOIC ERA. These are the two divisions of the Cryptozoic (hidden life) Era and are often designated as subdivisions of Pre-Cambrian time.      A. P. M.
SEE ALSO: GEOLOGIC TIME TABLE, ROCKS

**Archimedes** (287?–212 B.C.) (Are-kih-ME-deez) Archimedes was a Greek scientist and mathematician. He is famous for his work in geometry, physics and mechanics.

He discovered a principle, known today as *Archimedes' principle,* which states that a solid object when immersed in a liquid is buoyed up by a force equal to the weight of the displaced liquid. It is said that Ar-

※ **THINGS TO DO**

**PRINCIPLE: AN OBJECT IN A LIQUID IS BUOYED UP BY A FORCE EQUAL TO THE WEIGHT OF THE LIQUID IT DISPLACES**

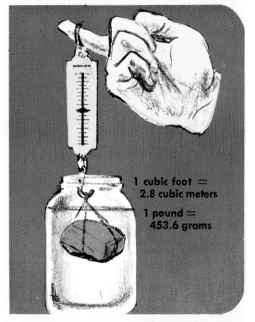

1 cubic foot = 2.8 cubic meters
1 pound = 453.6 grams

**Weigh a rock with a spring scale. Put it in a jar of water. One cubic foot of fresh water weighs about 62.3 pounds. How much does the rock weigh now? What is the buoyant force on the rock?**

chimedes discovered this principle in a most unusual way. The king of Syracuse suspected his goldsmith of dishonestly mixing silver with the gold for the royal crown. He commanded Archimedes to discover whether the crown was of pure gold. Archimedes pondered how he could measure the gold in the crown without actually melting it down. The answer came to him as he lowered himself into the tub at one of the public baths in Syracuse. He noticed that a certain amount of water spilled over the sides of the tub. Excitedly he realized that he had discovered the way to fulfill the king's command. He realized that the apparent loss of weight of an object immersed in water must be equal to the weight of the water displaced by the object. Why not use the same principle to find the amount of gold in the crown? Since gold and silver are of different densities, each would show a different apparent weight when immersed in water. A pure gold crown im-

**THINGS TO DO**

PRINCIPLE: DECREASING
DISPLACEMENT WILL DECREASE
THE BUOYANT FORCE. AIR MAY
BE COMPRESSED BUT WATER CAN
BE COMPRESSED ONLY SLIGHTLY

**1** Turn a small bottle upside down in a large bottle of water. Push down on the cork of the big bottle.

**2** Water forces the air inside the inverted floating bottle to become compressed. The volume of water displaced by the bottle is decreased. The buoyant force is decreased and the bottle goes to the bottom. When the cork is lifted the opposite occurs. The bottle rises to the surface.

mersed in water would weigh more than one of the same volume containing silver. The experiment was carried out and the goldsmith was found guilty.

Archimedes was the inventor of some of the most devastating machines of war known to his age. The siege of Syracuse by the Romans lasted three years chiefly because of the genius of Archimedes. Archimedes met an untimely death when Syracuse was finally captured by the Romans.  D. H. J.

**Archipelago** (ark-eh-PELL-uh-go) An archipelago is either a large body of water containing many ISLANDS or the group of islands itself. For example, the Aleutian Islands west of Alaska form an archipelago.

**Arctic** (ARK-tick) The area of the Arctic lies within the Arctic Circle and its center is the North Pole. Most of this region is covered by the Arctic Ocean, but it does include the northern parts of North America, Asia, and a small part of Europe. A large part of this area is covered by ice all year. Places that are near the Arctic Circle (66½ ° N. Lat.) have a very short growing season. This is the TUNDRA with its mosses, grasses, and low shrubs.

Of the islands near the Arctic Circle, only those with mean temperatures of not more than 50° F (10° C.) in summer and 32° F. (0° C.) in winter are called *arctic*. Surface travel is generally easier over frozen terrain, during winter; but in summer, surface melting makes travel difficult. Thus modern exploration was begun by water. ROALD AMUNDSEN of Norway first discovered a northwest passage (1903-1906). James Ross located the *magnetic north pole* in 1831; ROBERT PEARY reached the *geographic north pole* in 1909. Since then, most land masses have been charted. Scientists are now mapping the ocean floor and operating weather stations on drifting ice islands.

Small salt lakes open up during summer in the Arctic Ocean. In August, 1958, the U.S. nuclear submarine *Skate* surfaced nine times in such lakes. During winter, even these salt lakes may freeze; but in March, 1959, the *Skate* broke through the ice cap at the Pole.

The Arctic has special importance because many *great circle* aircraft routes cross it. It is militarily vital because the United States' *Distant Early Warning* system

**The Arctic Zone includes the northern tips of three continents plus many islands**

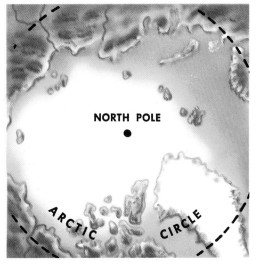

NORTH POLE

ARCTIC CIRCLE

(DEW line) has a series of aircraft and missile detectors across the Canadian and Alaskan Arctic.

Arctic waters are rich in crabs, jellyfish, and plankton, so fishes, seals and whales are abundant. The land yields valuable minerals, including uranium ores.　　E.R.B.

SEE ALSO: EARTH, POLES

### Arcturus  see Boötes

**Area** Area is the amount of surface included within a boundary. A measurement, usually expressed in square units, may be assigned to the area.

**Argon** Argon is a colorless, odorless, rather rare GAS found in the atmosphere. It makes up almost 1% of the air breathed. It is chemically inactive, so it does not form compounds with other elements. Its chief use is in the manufacture of electric light bulbs.

When an element combines with oxygen a chemical change takes place called *oxidation*. When a metal oxidizes it is in reality burning. However, for a metal to oxidize it must have oxygen with which to combine. Also, when metals are heated they become chemically more active. Therefore a TUNGSTEN filament in an electric light bulb would deteriorate rapidly if any oxygen were present. Argon, because it will not combine with tungsten, is an excellent gas to use in the inside of an electric light bulb.

Sir William Ramsay and Lord Rayleigh discovered argon in 1894. Its name, in Greek, means "the lazy one." It is prepared by cooling and compressing purified air until it becomes liquid. The argon is then separated by distillation and put into tanks for sale.

Argon (symbol A) is element number 18. It has an atomic weight of 39.948, I. K. F.

SEE ALSO: ATOM, ELEMENTS

**ARGONAUT**

**Argonaut** An argonaut is a tentacled female saltwater shellfish related to the OCTOPUS. The male lacks a shell. Another name is *paper nautilus*.

SEE ALSO: MOLLUSCA

**Arid** Arid means dry or lacking in moisture. Some arid land is DESERT.

Aries is an autumn constellation

**Aries** (AIR-eez) Aries, or The Ram, is a CONSTELLATION. It is the first sign of the ZODIAC. The Ram can be seen about midnight from June to February. But the best time to look for it is in the autumn. The three main stars of this group form a small curve. The stars of Aries are not as bright as some of the stars of other constellations.

Long ago the Babylonians, the Hebrews, the Persians, and the Arabs noticed this small group of stars and they all called it the Ram. Part of the Greek myth of the Golden Fleece explains (they thought) how the Ram got in the sky. The king of Thessaly had two sons, Phrixus and Helles. Their stepmother treated them badly. Mercury, a god, felt so sorry for the boys that he sent a ram with golden fleece to rescue them. Phrixus and Helles were to hold onto the ram's golden fleece while he flew them through the air. But when they were crossing the Hellespont, Helles lost his grip for a minute. He fell into the sea and drowned. That is how the Hellespont got its name. The ram did carry Phrixus to safety, however. Phrixus was so grateful to the gods for his escape that he sacrificed the ram to the gods. Jupiter, the king of the gods, gave the ram a place in the stars in recognition of what he did for Phrixus.　　C. L. K.

Aristotle was a scientist, philosopher and teacher. In his "peripatetic" school, he and his pupils strolled around as they talked

**Aristotle** (AHR-eh-stot-uhl) Aristotle was a Greek scientist and teacher. He was the first person to study BIOLOGY —the science of life. He collected the first library in Europe, and he gathered together animals for the first zoo. These animals were sent to him by Alexander the Great's soldiers.

Born in Stagira in the remote northeast, in Thrace, Aristotle was the son of the court physician to the king of Macedonia. His father was one of his early tutors, giving him a sound education in the natural sciences. At the age of seventeen he was sent to Athens to complete his education at Plato's Academy. He studied under the great Plato for twenty years and was strongly influenced by his thinking. Plato called Aristotle's house "the house of the reader" because Aristotle had collected a large number of parchment scrolls. In fact, his was the first library in Europe. Aristotle was interested in all areas of knowledge known in his time. He was the first biologist. In addition, he was the first person to study all forms of life with an aim to classifying living creatures according to a system. This classification has been called his *scala natura*, a Latin term meaning "natural scale."

After the death of Plato, Aristotle was invited to tutor Alexander, the fourteen-year-old son of the king of Macedonia. This relationship lasted only a few years, but there seems to be evidence that Alexander did not forget his former teacher, who had taught him "the art of living." In fact, after Alexander had inherited his father's throne and had set off on his Asian expedition, he ordered several thousands of his men to collect rare specimens of animal and plant life and, together with the observations they had made, ship them back to Aristotle. By this time Aristotle had returned to Athens and was busily engaged in using these specimens to organize a great zoological garden which Alexander seems to have designed and financed.

In addition, Aristotle established his famous school known as the Peripatetic school of philosophy. The word *peripatetic* is a Greek word meaning to walk around. And this is exactly what Aristotle and his pupils did! Together they strolled along the shaded walks of the Lyceum while he talked with them. It is thought that Aristotle composed here most of his known works on natural science, metaphysics, logic, ethics, politics, rhetoric, and poetics.

In 323 B.C., the year of Alexander's death, Aristotle was forced to flee Athens to a nearby Macedonian garrison. Alexander's death had released a strong surge of anti-Macedonian feeling which had built up during the period of Macedonian leadership, and Aristotle was accused of "godlessness." Exile affected him keenly and he died within the year.

Aristotle's primary interest was to answer the question, "What is the good life for man?" He reasoned that if he could observe each living thing and make complete records of his observations, he would be close to understanding life. His observations began with marine life and progressed to mammals. He worked under great handicaps, having no books to consult, no scientific instruments to use, and no one with whom he could discuss his findings. In spite of these hardships, Aristotle made countless contributions to science that later were verified. Others are still being argued. D. H. J.

**Arithmetic** (uh-RITH-muh-tick) Arithmetic is a system of concepts and processes which man has created to determine, to record, and to communicate ideas of number and number relationships. Since it is used to think about and to exchange ideas of quantity, it functions also as a language and as a means of arriving at answers to certain kinds of mathematical questions. Because the Hindu-Arabic system of notation is used throughout the civilized world, arithmetic concerns itself with the ten digits—1, 2, 3, 4, 5, 6, 7, 8, 9, 0—and the fundamental operations as applied to this system.

The basic idea underlying arithmetic is *counting*. Counting requires an understanding of the *cardinal* (grouping) meaning of number, as well as an awareness of the *ordinal* (ordering) meaning of number. When symbols such as 2, 5, 7 are used to indicate "how many in all"—like "two," "five," "seven"—they are being used in their cardinal sense. When symbols such as 2, 5, 7 denote position in a series and convey the idea of "second," "fifth," "seventh," they are used in their ordinal sense.

The cardinal number is a property common to all sets of things that have the same amount of elements. Names and symbols are used to express this property. The word three and the symbol 3 express this property for all sets of things that have this amount of elements. Some earlier people represented the number "3" as: ||| (Egyptian), ϒ (Greek), ≡ (Chinese), and III (Roman).

Throughout the ages people have used different symbols to name numbers. They also have invented different systems of numeration—that is, different ways of using these symbols to express numbers. Our system, the Hindu-Arabic system, is a decimal system (base 10) because the grouping is done by 10. It is also a positional system because the position in which a digit appears determines its value. The numeral 63 stands for 6 tens and 3 ones, whereas the numeral 36 stands for 3 tens and 6 ones. The numeral 603 stands for 6 hundreds, 0 tens, and 3 ones, or (6 x 100) + (0 x 10) + (3 x 1).

In the Egyptian system of notation, a vertical staff ( | ) stood for 1, a heel bone (∩) for 10, a scroll for 100, a lotus flower for 1000, a pointing finger for 10,000, a fish for 100,000 and a man in astonishment for 1,000,000. This system was decimal but not positional. Any symbol could be used as many as nine times, but if ten of that particular symbol were needed, the Egyptians used a new symbol. The number 63 was expressed as ∩∩∩ ∩∩∩ |||; the number 60 as ∩∩∩ ∩∩∩ . Note that there is no symbol to tell there are no ones, such as the zero in the Hindu-Arabic system.

The Babylonians had a system employing positional notation, but their system was not decimal. It was a sexagesimal system (base 60) because the grouping was by sixties. The number 63 was expressed ▼ ▼▼▼. The space between the first ▼ and the next three ▼ indicated that the first ▼ stood for 60. This system also did not have a symbol for zero; thus, ▼ alone could mean 1 or 60.

It is then possible for a system of notation to be decimal but not positional, as in the case of the Egyptian, and positional but not decimal as in the Babylonian.

Arithmetic has developed as a functional

| | HINDU DIGITS (1050 A.D.) | | | | | | | | |
|---|---|---|---|---|---|---|---|---|---|
| 0 | 1 | 2 | 3 | 4 | 5 | 6 | 7 | 8 | 9 |

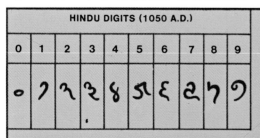

Hindu digits are base 10, or decimal. The position of the digits is important in deciding what the digit's value. For example, the digit 7 can stand for 7 ones (7), 7 tens (70), 7 hundreds (700), etc.

| EGYPTIAN HIEROGLYPHICS | | | | | | |
|---|---|---|---|---|---|---|
| 1 | 10 | 100 | 1,000 | 10,000 | 100,000 | 1,000,000 |

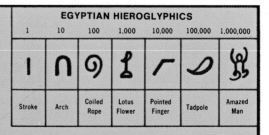

| Stroke | Arch | Coiled Rope | Lotus Flower | Pointed Finger | Tadpole | Amazed Man |
|---|---|---|---|---|---|---|

In hieroglyphics, the digit system is also decimal, but position is not as important. Instead, each symbol can be used up to 9 times. To show 7 tens, the Egyptians would draw 7 arches; 7 hundreds would be shown as 7 coiled ropes, etc.

tool designed to meet mankind's increasing quantitative needs. In the past century mathematicians have attempted to state the basic laws of arithmetic as a logical structure. These are often called *axioms*.

Arithmetic consists of a set of elements, called numbers and operations. The set of numbers in arithmetic problems may differ from time to time. The concern may be only the positive whole numbers (1, 2, 3 . . . ) At other times, the set under consideration may be the positive common or decimal fractions (such as $\frac{2}{3}$, $\frac{1}{4}$, .33. . . , .25), or it may be the set of integers (positive and negative whole numbers.)

There are two binary operations, called *addition* and *multiplication,* designated by the symbols + and ×. A binary operation is one which can be performed on only two numbers at a time. Interestingly enough, it is possible to add only two numbers at a time or to multiply only two numbers at a time. To be able to multiply three numbers such as 3 × 4 × 5, one must find the product of 3 and 4 and then multiply this by 5.

$$3 \times 4 = 12 \quad 12 \times 5 = 60$$
$$3 \times 4 \times 5 = 60$$

The basic laws for the arithmetic of a set of numbers and the two operations, addition and multiplication, are:

It is always possible to add any two numbers or to multiply any two numbers, and the result shall be an arithmetic number.
$3 + 7 = 10$; $8 \times 7 = 56$; $\frac{1}{3} + \frac{2}{5} = 1\frac{1}{15}$; $\frac{1}{3} \times \frac{2}{5} = \frac{2}{15}$; $.16 \times 1.4 = .224$

Any two numbers can have only one sum. Any two numbers can have only one product.

3 + 7 equals 10 and only 10
8 × 7 equals 56 and only 56

The order of addition or multiplication of two numbers does not affect the outcome.
$$3 + 7 = 7 + 3 ; 8 \times 7 = 7 \times 8$$

When three numbers are involved, the grouping of the numbers does not affect the result.

$$3 + 7 + 9 = 3 + (7 + 9) = (3 + 7) + 9$$

$$2 \times 3 \times 5 = 2 \times (3 \times 5) = (2 \times 3) \times 5$$

Multiplication is distributive over addition. This axiom can best be explained by an example.

$$3 \times 14 = 3 \times (10 + 4) =$$
$$(3 \times 10) + (3 \times 4) = 30 + 12 = 42$$

The value of any number is unchanged when zero (0) is added to it. When any number is multiplied by 1, the product is equivalent to that number.
$$7 + 0 = 7 \qquad 4 \times 1 = 4$$
For every number (except 0) there is an inverse for multiplication, its reciprocal. The reciprocal of 3 is $\frac{1}{3}$. The reciprocal of $\frac{1}{5}$ is 5. The reciprocal of $\frac{3}{4}$ is $\frac{4}{3}$.

Suppose that for each of these two operations there exists an "undoing" operation which brings one right back to the starting point. The number 4 added to the number 3 yields the sum 7. The number 7 "undone" by the number 4 yields the number 3. This inverse (undoing) operation is called *subtraction*. One writes $7 - 4 = 3$ and says "Seven minus four is three." One also says that the difference obtained when 4 is subtracted from 7 is 3. Notice that $7 - 4 = 3$, because $3 + 4 = 7$. When 3 is multiplied by 4 the product is 12, or $4 \times 3 = 12$. Assuming the inverse operation exists for multiplication, it is possible to take the number 12, operate on it with the number 4, and get the number 3. This inverse operation is called *division*. One writes $12 \div 4 = 3$ and says "Twelve divided by four is three." Again, $12 \div 4 = 3$ because $4 \times 3 = 12$.

The so-called four fundamental operations of arithmetic are illustrated as mathematical statements or questions:

Addition: 3 + 7 = ☐
Subtraction: 14 − 9 = ☐ or 14 = 9 + ☐
Multiplication: 3 × 7 = ☐
Division: 24 ÷ 3 = ☐ or 3 × ☐ = 24
In each of these examples, the ☐ stands for a number.

The *algorithms,* routine procedures for computing, follow logically from the properties of our number system and the basic laws.

Arithmetic has a wide variety of applications. Our world is full of numbers and amounts to be quantified and problems involving these. Arithmetic helps mankind deal with these problems in a logical, organized, and efficient manner. M.M.L./I.K.F.

SEE ALSO: ALGEBRA, MATHEMATICS

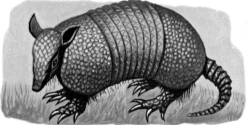

**Armadillo**

**Armadillo** The armadillo is a mammal covered by its own "armor" for protection. The armor is made of a hard bony substance. When in danger, the animal can roll into a ball. The armadillo is also protected by strong claws. It moves about mostly at night and eats insects, roots, and fruits.

The home of the armadillo is a burrow which it can dig quickly with its powerful claws. Armadillos range in size from only a few inches or centimeters up to about 4 feet (1.22 meters), but fossils of even larger forms have been found. They live mainly in South America, but some live in the southern part of the United States.

The young are born large and tough-skinned, and, unlike most mammals, they are able to see at birth. As they grow, the armor plates become solidified. *Armadillo* is a Spanish word meaning "little armored one." M. E. C.

**Armament** see Missile, Rocket, Weapons

**Armature** (AHR-mah-ture) An armature consists of many turns of insulated wire wound around a piece of soft iron. It is the armature of an electric DYNAMO or generator in which electrical energy is induced.

When a coil of wire through which a current is running is wound around an iron bar, a magnet and a magnetic field are produced for the time the current is running. When a

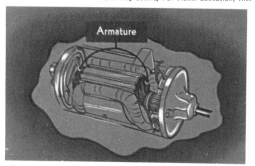

Armature

magnetic field is cut by a wire, or cuts across a wire, a current is induced in the wire if the circuit is closed. This discovery of MICHAEL FARADAY in 1831 is at the heart of the electric generator. It is called electromagnetic INDUCTION.

In the direct current electric motor the magnetic force which operates between the armature and the field magnet causes the armature to rotate when the current passes through the armature. In the *direct current generator* the rotation of the armature causes the current to flow through the stationary field.

In an *alternating current generator* the field moves past the stationary coils of the armature. In the huge alternating current generators in use today the field magnet *(rotor)* rotates while the generating coils on the armature *(stator)* are stationary.

The armature in a generator may be turned by the power derived from coal, coke, gasoline, or falling water. I. K. F.

SEE ALSO: ELECTRICITY, ELECTROMAGNET

**Arnica** Arnica is a group of yellow-flowered herbs of the THISTLE family which grows in the northern hemisphere.

SEE: HERB

**Arrowroot** Arrowroot is a STARCH made from the RHIZOMES (underground stems) of several tropical HERBS. Since it is easily digested, it is often used in baby foods.

SEE: CARBOHYDRATE, STEMS

**Arsenic** Arsenic is a chemical element. Compounds of it can quickly kill many insects that destroy garden plants. Small amounts of it will make some metals harden. But, when wrongly used, arsenic chemicals are slowly poisonous to man.

Arsenic (symbol As) is element number 33. It has an atomic weight of 74.9216 (74.91, $O = 16$). When pure, it is a steel-gray solid. It is not found free in nature. It occurs mainly in the dark red sulfide realgar ($As_2S_2$) and arsenic-iron pyrites ($FeSAs$). Two of its important compounds used as INSECTICIDES are Paris green ($CuHAsO_3$) and lead arsenate [$Pb_3(AsO_4)_2$]. D. A. B.

SEE ALSO: ATOM, ELEMENTS, POISON

**Arteriosclerosis** (are-TEAR-ee-oh-skleer-OH-sis) Arteriosclerosis describes a condition that may develop in the arteries, the vessels that carry the blood away from the heart. As people grow older their blood vessels become less elastic and do not contract and expand as easily as they did when younger. This is known as *hardening of the arteries* or arteriosclerosis.

In arteriosclerosis, there are deposits of fatty substances and, in a later stage, of calcium within the arterial walls. Improper METABOLISM of fats are believed to be responsible for the CHOLESTEROL deposits that harden and thicken the vessels.

People who have *hypertension* or high BLOOD PRESSURE and are obese are often victims of arteriosclerosis. They may suffer from poor circulation, heart attacks, strokes, or kidney diseases.      J. D. B.
SEE ALSO: ARTERY, CIRCULATORY SYSTEM

**Artery** Arteries are tubes which carry blood from the heart to all parts of the body. In man, a large artery leads from each of two chambers (ventricles) of the heart. The arteries grow smaller and smaller as they branch out and reach all parts of the body. These *arterioles* (small arteries) branch into the *capillaries,* the smallest tubes in the blood system. They in turn enlarge into venioles and VEINS. The veins return the blood to the heart. This completes the circle the blood takes through the body.

The *pulmonary* artery leaves the right ventricle and branches into two arteries, one going to each lung. These arteries carry blood with an excess of carbon dioxide, a waste to be eliminated. The *aorta* leads out of the left ventricle and arches back over the heart. It is one inch in diameter and has very thick walls. It begins the work of carrying food and oxygen to all parts of the body.

The beating of the HEART propels blood through the arteries. The artery walls contract and expand to accommodate the flow

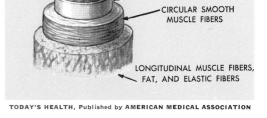

MEDIUM-SIZED ARTERY
ENDOTHELIUM
ELASTIC MEMBRANE
CIRCULAR SMOOTH MUSCLE FIBERS
LONGITUDINAL MUSCLE FIBERS, FAT, AND ELASTIC FIBERS

TODAY'S HEALTH, Published by AMERICAN MEDICAL ASSOCIATION

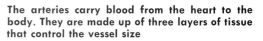

The arteries carry blood from the heart to the body. They are made up of three layers of tissue that control the vessel size

of blood. This artery wall movement is called *pulse.* It can be felt inside the wrist and at other points on the body where an artery lies close to the surface.

Artery walls have three distinct layers. The outer coat is an elastic connective tissue which provides resilience under pressure. The middle layer is composed of smooth muscle, which can change the size of the vessel opening and therefore the amount of blood it can carry. The inner layer is a thin membrane lined with smooth cells which reduce friction as the blood flows through the artery.

The word *artery* means "air pipe." Arteries were so named because of the ancient belief that air rather than blood passes through the body.      I. H. S.
SEE ALSO: CIRCULATORY SYSTEM

### Artesian well see Well

**Arthritis** Arthritis is an inflammation of the joints, causing aching, painful, swollen, and stiff joints. It may be caused by disease, injury, or degeneration.

Many diseases have arthritis as part of their symptoms. Some of these are tuberculosis, syphilis, pneumonia, rheumatic fever, gonorrhea, dysentery, and gout.

Infected teeth or tonsils may sometimes act as *foci of infection* and secondarily cause painful joints. Removal of the infection may cure the condition. A skin disease called *psoriasis* may cause painful joints. SICKLE CELL ANEMIA and HEMOPHILIA may cause swollen joints by bleeding into them.

Bacteria and viruses may invade the joints and produce swelling with fever, redness, and PUS formation. More often, however, joint fluid is found to be sterile (without organisms). Then the swelling is thought to be due to an allergy to oneself or an old injury. Anti-inflammatory drugs such as aspirin are useful, and CORTISONE injected into the joint (or occasionally in severe cases given by mouth) dramatically reduces swelling and pain.

*Rheumatoid* arthritis is an example of painful joints where no bacteria or infection can be found in the joints. The cause is unknown. The condition affects symmetrical joints—if the knuckles of one hand are swollen and painful the knuckles of the other hand will probably be, too. This condition can lead to great crippling.

RHEUMATIC FEVER can produce swelling, redness, and heat in a joint. Often the pain in one joint will pass rapidly and involve another joint (migratory arthritis). This condition occurs in a small percentage of people who have a streptococcal infection (usually of the throat) which is not treated with antibiotics. When the condition ends, the joints will be entirely normal, but the heart may have been affected. Complete bed rest may help prevent heart damage.

GOUT is a painful joint condition due to the body's overproduction of and/or inability to metabolize PURINES and uric acid. Too much uric acid in the bloodstream can crystallize in the kidneys, damaging them, or in a joint (often the big toe), causing extreme tenderness, swelling, and redness. Diet is a factor in management, but drugs to reduce the swelling and pain or to lower the amount of uric acid in the blood are more useful. E.S.S./B.M.H.

SEE ALSO: JOINTS, SKELETON, ALLERGY

**Arthropoda** Arthropods are a very large group of animals with jointed legs. A joint is important to an animal. It joins two parts of the body and allows these parts to bend. A person would not be able to run, skip or jump if his legs and feet did not bend at the joints.

Arthropods are able to walk instead of crawl. The legs are under the body. They lift the body off the ground, so that the arthropod is able to move very fast. The joints allow greater freedom of motion.

Most arthropods are well known. Lobsters, shrimp, crabs, spiders, insects, mites, ticks, centipedes, and millipedes are some animals in this group.

These animals are very successful in this world. Some live in the ooze at the bottom of the ocean. Some fly through the air. Others are found in fresh water, on land and in soil. They are found in most parts of the world. They eat the largest number of plants and animals. They eat the most un-

**Phylum *Arthropoda* is the largest and most varied group of animals. The delicate and usually harmless katydid (lower left) belongs to Class *Insecta*. The large, hairy tarantula (lower right) belongs to Class *Arachnida***

Buchsbaum

Buchsbaum

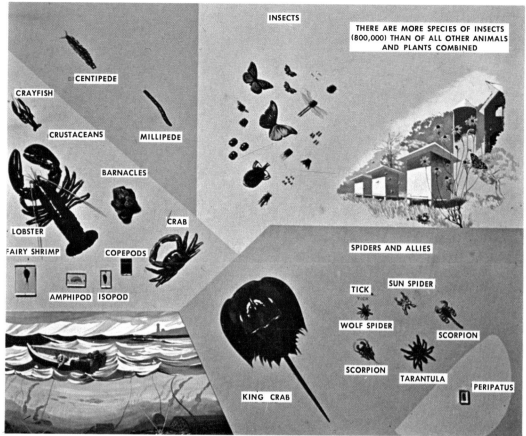

INSECTS

THERE ARE MORE SPECIES OF INSECTS (800,000) THAN OF ALL OTHER ANIMALS AND PLANTS COMBINED

CENTIPEDE

CRAYFISH

CRUSTACEANS

MILLIPEDE

BARNACLES

CRAB

LOBSTER

FAIRY SHRIMP

COPEPODS

AMPHIPOD   ISOPOD

SPIDERS AND ALLIES

TICK   SUN SPIDER

WOLF SPIDER

SCORPION

SCORPION   TARANTULA

PERIPATUS

KING CRAB

Chicago Natural History Museum

usual foods, such as cloth and wooden buildings. They have special body parts for protection against their enemies. Their thick outer skeleton is made of a material called CHITIN. It protects the soft body underneath. Different animals have pincers, large eyes, antennae, stingers, and poison claws. Arthropods are so successful, that four-fifths of all the known animals in the world are members of the group.

Many of the larger animals depend upon arthropods as food. Since many arthropods feed upon plants, they change large amounts of the plant protoplasm into useable food for other animals. For example, insects are food for such animals as fish, birds and reptiles. Lobster, shrimp and other aquatic animals are food for man.

Many arthropods are of great benefit to mankind. The hard-working BEES and other insects naturally cross-pollinate flowering plants. Silk is provided by the SILKWORM as well as the spider. However, other arthropods are harmful to mankind. Some

insects destroy fresh meat and plants. Blood-sucking mites and ticks transfer diseases. Arthropods are so numerous in many places that they make life difficult or even impossible for man.

An outer covering, or *exoskeleton,* of chitin protects the soft inner tissues of the arthropod. Chitin is as important to the arthropod as steel was to a knight in armor. This exoskeleton is constructed like a suit of armor. To enable a knight to bend his body, the suit of armor had to be made with moveable steel plates. The armor-like exoskeleton of the arthropod is composed of moveable chitinous plates.

In body structure, the arthropod may be compared to a passenger plane. On the inside, the plane is divided into many compartments, such as control rooms, passenger lounges and storage rooms. From the outside the plane appears to have only three main parts, the nose, the main body, and the tail sections. The outer structure does not reveal the inner structure. It would not be practical for a plane to be constructed in moveable sections, like those of a train. The three main sections are fused together so that they move together. In the same way,

141

Courtesy Society For Visual Education, Inc.

**A thousand kinds of crabs are in Class *Crustacea***

Courtesy Society For Visual Education, Inc.

**Honeybees (of Class *Insecta*) on a sumac branch**

the arthropod body consists of segments, or inner divisions, which are fused together to form three main outer body parts—the head, thorax, and the abdomen.

Several segments are fused together to form the head. Except for the first segment, each segment has a pair of jointed appendages, such as jaws for biting or sucking, antennae for feeling, or claws and mouth parts for capturing and ingesting food. Eyes are also located on the head. The simple and compound EYE may both appear on the same animal. The compound eye is unique to the arthropods. It is made up of many complete units, each with a separate lens.

The appendages for locomotion are located on the thorax. Each type of animal has a definite number of appendages. The arachnids—spiders, ticks and mites—have four pairs of walking legs, while the INSECTS have three pairs of walking legs and two pairs of wings. The abdomen usually contains the anal and reproductive openings. Appendages may also be present on the abdomen.

Arthropods have systems for transportation of messages or substances throughout the body. A brain and nerve cords make up the nervous system. The inner nervous system connects with outer sense organs, such as eyes, antennae, hearing organs, sensory bristles and hairs. A simple heart and a series of blood vessels leading into open spaces throughout the body make up the blood system. The digestive tube is lined at the mouth and anus with chitin. Digestion takes place in the middle section. Excretory organs often empty into the digestive tube. For breathing, most land arthropods have a system of tubes lined with chitin, which are called *trachea*. The tubes open to the surface and air circulates to the inner tissues. Most aquatic arthropods, like the lobster, have gills.

Among arthropods, the sexes are usually separate. Arthropods lay many eggs. Since the adult may develop within a few days or weeks, there may be several generations a year. All larva develop into adults by MOLTING their outer covering several times before they reach adulthood.     E. P. L.

SEE ALSO: ANIMAL; ANIMALS, CLASSIFICATION OF; ARACHNIDA; CRUSTACEA; INSECTA; METAMORPHOSIS; MILLIPEDE

**The centipede is in a class by itself**

Courtesy Society For Visual Education, Inc.

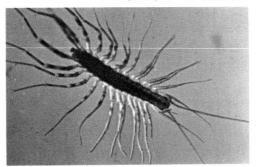

**The American locust is also of Class *Insecta***

Courtesy Society For Visual Education, Inc.

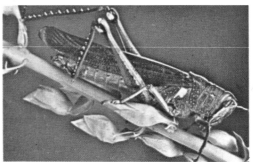

**Artichoke** The fleshy center of the flower bud is the part of the artichoke plant that is eaten as a vegetable. The tough outer part (the *bracts*) is discarded.

This perennial herb thrives in milder climates, as the rootstock of the true *burr* or *globe* artichoke does not survive cold weather. New plants are grown from sprouts rather than seeds.                    H. J. C.

**Artificial respiration** The breathing in of air and the breathing out of air is called *respiration*. In healthy animals with lungs this is automatic. In cases of drowning, strangling, poisoning by gases or drugs, electric shock, bulbar polio, and spinal cord injuries, normal respiration may stop. Then artificial respiration, which is the act of forcing air in and out of the lungs by external pressure, is necessary.

Many methods of administering artificial respiration have been developed. *Mouth-to-mouth breathing* is an effective way to revive a person who has suddenly stopped breathing. Everyone should know this procedure and not hesitate to use it when necessary. Do not be timid. The chance of catching infection from the victim is very small. When mouth-to-mouth breathing is properly done, the victim's breath is not inhaled by the rescuer. (*If the victim's heart has also stopped beating, then artificial respiration must be accompanied by closed chest cardiac massage—pressing rhythmically on the chest to restore an artificial circulation. This procedure is then called cardiopulmonary resuscitation or CPR.*)

Mouth-to-mouth breathing can be used in the water if necessary. When on land, place the victim on his back. Remove any secretions or obstructions to the air passage by sweeping the finger around the inside of the mouth (see A below). If a person has inhaled a large piece of food, do not strike him on the back. Have the person put his head down while you clear the food from the throat by hand. If this does not work, use the Heimlich Choke Maneuver. (For babies and small children, see B below.)

1. Elevate the chin by pulling it upward. At the same time, tilt the head backward and down so that the chin and neck protrude upward. This straightens and opens the passageway to the lungs.

2. Force the jaw forward by pressing upward on the angle of the jaw just below the ears. This brings the tongue out of the back of the throat.

3. Place your mouth over the victim's mouth and pinch the nostrils closed so that air cannot escape.

4. Blow your breath with force into the victim's mouth. His chest should rise.

5. Remove your mouth and push downward on his chest to assist in removing the air from his lungs. Repeat this 12-14 times in one minute. With a child, an adult's mouth will cover his nose as well, and there is no need to pinch the nostrils closed.

Breathe 20 times per minute for a child. If the victim's heart has stopped, the heart can be pressed 60 times per minute, with mouth-to-mouth breathing after every fifth compression.               E.S.S./B.M.H.

SEE ALSO: FIRST AID, HEIMLICH CHOKE MANEUVER, RESPIRATORY SYSTEM

**A: Remove any obstructions. Steps 1-5: See article.**

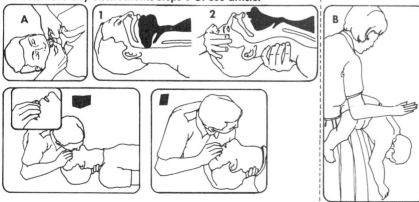

B. If a baby or small child inhales a piece of food, hold the victim head-down over your arm. Strike him sharply between the shoulder blades to jar obstructing material loose.

**Artiodactyla** (art-ee-o-DAK-tila) Animals that have a split hoof or an even number of toes are put into a new order of mammals called Artiodactyla. Cows, sheep, pigs, deer, camels, and hippopotamuses are in this group. They are often ruminants, which means they have several stomachs to digest their plant food.

Animals that have a single hoof on each foot or an odd number of toes are put into another order called *Perissodactyla.* This group includes rhinoceroses, horses, tapirs, and zebras. They usually have an elongated head, and some are fast runners.

Artiodactylas are found all over the world, whereas the perissodactylas inhabit America, Africa, and Asia. These animals were once grouped together in the order Ungulata. Many of these are becoming endangered species, especially in the African herds. H.J.C.

**Asbestos** Asbestos is a general name used for a group of minerals. The minerals occur in nature as soft, silky, flexible fibers. The fibers are easily separated. Once separated, the fibers can be woven into yarn. The yarn can be used to make heat- and fire-resistant materials.

Much evidence has been collected indicating that asbestos is a cause of cancer. Due to this danger, environmentalists suggest that man's contact with asbestos be minimal. A.J.H.

SEE ALSO: MINERAL

**Ascaris** (ASS-kuh-riss) Ascaris is a roundworm which is not segmented. It is a PARASITE, which means it lives in another living creature from whom it gets its food and shelter. The ascaris is found in the intestines of man and domesticated animals. They are uninvited guests that set up housekeeping in the intestines, entering the body through the mouth. These worms come from infected beef, pork, fish, vegetables, or water supplies. A doctor can treat a person who has discovered roundworms in the bowel movements. Certain drugs will kill the worms and the eggs.

A human being or other animal can become infested with roundworms by eating food that has been contaminated with the eggs or the adult of the roundworm. The worms will live in the intestinal canal and the eggs will hatch into worms and live, grow, and reproduce. The larvae sometimes pass through the intestinal wall into the venous system and cause lung inflammation.

The worm that infects humans is called *Ascaris lumbircoides.* About 3 million people in North America are infected by this worm.

When a person has roundworms, there are few symptoms unless he has a great number of worms. Worms are no disgrace but they need treatment. The most important treatment, however, is prevention. Many thousands of lives have been spared of worms because of proper disposal of sewage and garbage. Careful inspection of cattle and foods, and thorough washing and cooking of vegetables and meats have helped to decrease the number of worm-infested people and animals. J. K. K.

SEE ALSO: NEMATHELMINTHES

**Ascorbic acid** see Vitamin

**Asexual reproduction** see Reproduction, asexual

**Ash** The ash is a tall tree which grows from 40 to 80 feet (12.2 to 24.4 meters) high. The wood is light reddish-brown in color. Many leaflets

**Ash tree and leaf**

make up one leaf. It flowers in late spring. The fruit is winged and dry. It has only one seed.

There are thirty-nine different kinds or species of ash trees, such as the red, black, blue, green, and white ash. Ash trees belong to the OLIVE family.

Ash wood is widely used because it is strong and hard, yet lightweight and flexible. There is ash wood in baseball bats, snowshoes, garden tools, bowling alleys, bushel baskets, handles, and in many other things that require a hard, tough wood. Ash logs will burn while they are still green because the sap in the wood is flammable.

J.D.B.

**Asia** Asia is the largest continent on earth. It covers one-third of the land area of the world. EUROPE, which is counted as a separate continent, is really connected to Asia like a huge peninsula. More than half of the people of the world live in Asia.

There are five major types of climates on earth; all can be found in Asia. This is mainly due to the great north-south extent of this huge landmass. Asia has some of the world's coldest temperatures and the most rainfall in the Northern Hemisphere.

About half of Asia consists of bleak plateaus and high mountains. Mount Everest, over 29,000 feet (8,839 meters) high, is the highest mountain on earth.

Asia faces three oceans—on the north, the Arctic; on the east, the Pacific; and on the south, the Indian Ocean. On the Pacific side, where there are branching land formations and islands, the arms of the ocean are designated as seas. Among these are the South China Sea, the Sea of Japan, and the Sea of Okhotsk. Asia has nearly 50,000 miles (80,467

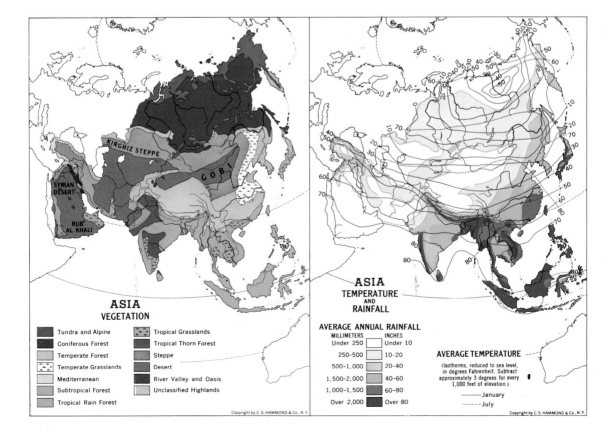

**ASIA**
VEGETATION

- Tundra and Alpine
- Coniferous Forest
- Temperate Forest
- Temperate Grasslands
- Mediterranean
- Subtropical Forest
- Tropical Rain Forest
- Tropical Grasslands
- Tropical Thorn Forest
- Steppe
- Desert
- River Valley and Oasis
- Unclassified Highlands

Copyright by C.S. HAMMOND & Co., N.Y.

**ASIA**
TEMPERATURE
AND
RAINFALL

**AVERAGE ANNUAL RAINFALL**

| MILLIMETERS | INCHES |
|---|---|
| Under 250 | Under 10 |
| 250-500 | 10-20 |
| 500-1,000 | 20-40 |
| 1,500-2,000 | 40-60 |
| 1,000-1,500 | 60-80 |
| Over 2,000 | Over 80 |

**AVERAGE TEMPERATURE**

(Isotherms, reduced to sea level, in degrees Fahrenheit. Subtract approximately 3 degrees for every 1,000 feet of elevation.)

— January
------- July

Copyright by C.S. HAMMOND & Co., N.Y.

kilometers) of coast line, much of it making good harbors.

## LAND FORMS

The continent of Asia extends from the equator to 80° north LATITUDE (N. Lat.) although some of the Asian islands extend to 10° S. Lat. In LONGITUDE, Asia extends from about 27° E. to 170° W. The area of Asia is about 18,000,000 square miles (46,619,820 square kilometers).

The mountain chains of central Asia are tremendous. From this central point of the great Pamirs, the Hindu Kush range extends westward through Afghanistan. Elevations are as great as 20,000 feet (6,096 meters.)

Eastward from the Pamirs, the impressive mountain system branches in several directions. The Karakoram arches north and the Himalayas southward. There is also a shorter range of the Himalayas lying east and west. Many mountain peaks are nearly as high as Mount Everest, and even the passes through these mountains are at elevations of 14,000 feet (4,267 meters) or more. Mountains branch off into southeastern Asia and China. Northeastward the mountains form a boundary of Outer Mongolia and extend into Siberia.

The Tibetan plateau lies at an elevation of about 16,000 feet (4,877 meters), but the Mongolian plateau is not more than 5,000 feet (1,524 meters) high. Plateaus are numerous over the continent. Asia has seven major plateaus, including the Dekkan in India, the Anatolian in Turkey, the Arabian, and the Iranian. Hill country is often associated with plateau regions. South China is a hilly region. India and southwestern Asia contain many foothills.

## CLIMATE

Asia's climate presents great contrasts both in temperature and the amount of annual precipitation received. Much of southern Asia has a tropical rain forest climate where the yearly temperature variation is only about 1°, and the total rainfall is more than 60 inches (152 centimeters.) Extreme northern Asia has a subpolar climate with a large yearly temperature range and little rain.

The tropical *monsoon* climate of Asia is located to the north of the tropical rain forests. Parts of India, China, Myanmar (Burma), and Thailand experience this cli-

mate. This type of climate is caused by the "monsoon effect," which is a seasonal change in the direction of the prevailing winds. In the summer, when the land is warmer than the ocean, heavy monsoon rains occur.

As these land areas begin to warm in the early spring, they develop lower air pressure than the surrounding Indian Ocean. This causes cooler, moisture-laden winds to blow inland where heavy rains may fall for five to eight months. In the dry season these conditions are exactly reversed. High pressure develops overland and flows outward.

Chicago Natural History Museum

**The sloth bear of India**

Chicago Natural History Museum

**The takin of China is related to the goats**

Chicago Natural History Museum

**The seladang is a wild buffalo found in the forests of Indo-China**

# ASIA

| 0 | 500 | 1000 | 1500 MI. |
|---|---|---|---|
| 0 | 500 | 1000 | 1500 KM. |

NORTH AMERICA

PACIFIC

ATLANTIC OCEAN

North Pole

Cape Dezhnev

BERING SEA

0° 20° 40° 60° 80° 100° 120° 140° 160° 180°

ARCTIC OCEAN

Cape Chelyuskin

Arctic Circle

Kamchatka Pen.

SIBERIA

EUROPE

RUSSIA

Siberia

SEA OF OKHOTSK

KURIL IS.

Moscow

Yekaterinburg

Ural Mountains

OB

YENISEY

LENA

AMUR

40°

Omsk    Novosibirsk

Chelyabinsk

IRTYSH

OB

Irkutsk

LAKE BAYKAL

Vladivostok

SEA OF JAPAN

Honshu

PACIFIC OCEAN

BLACK SEA

Ankara

TURKEY

CYPRUS
LEBANON
SYRIA
ISRAEL
JORDAN

URAL

KAZAKHSTAN

ARAL SEA

CASPIAN SEA

Ulaanbaatar

MONGOLIA

Gobi

Shenyang

HE  Beijing

Tianjin

N. KOREA

Seoul

S. KOREA

Tokyo

Osaka

RYUKYU IS.

40°

Tashkent

Alma-Ata

Ürümqi

Tian Shan

UZBEKISTAN

TURKMENISTAN

KYRGYZSTAN

TAJIKISTAN

Tehran

IRAN

IRAQ

Baghdad

KUWAIT

AFGHANISTAN

Islamabad

INDUS

Kunlun Shan

HUANG

CHINA

Lanzhou

HUANG (YANGTZE)

CHANG

JIANG

Wuhan

Shanghai

North Tropic Line (Tropic of Cancer)

20°

SAUDI

Riyadh

Mecca

BAH.

QATAR

UNITED ARAB EMIRATES

OMAN

Lahore

PAKISTAN

New Delhi

Himalaya

NEPAL

Tibet

Mt. Everest
29,028 ft (8848 m)

Chongqing

Guangzhou

HONG KONG
(U.K.)

TAIWAN

RED SEA

ARABIA

YEMEN

GULF OF ADEN

Karachi

GANGES

BANGLADESH

BU.

Hanoi

BURMA

LAOS

SOUTH CHINA SEA

Manila

PHILIPPINES

AFRICA

ARABIAN SEA

Bombay

Hyderabad

Madras

INDIA

Calcutta

BAY OF BENGAL

Rangoon

THAILAND

Bangkok

VIETNAM

CAMBODIA

Ho Chi Minh City

MEKONG

0°

SEYCHELLES

Cape Comorin

SRI LANKA
(CEYLON)

Colombo

MALDIVES

Malay

MALAYSIA

BRUNEI

Celebes

0°

INDIAN

Kuala Lumpur

Pen.

SINGAPORE

Borneo

INDONESIA

OCEAN

Equator

SUNDA

Sumatra

Java    Surabaya

Timor

BRITISH INDIAN OCEAN TERRITORY

Jakarta

ISLANDS

20°

Madagascar

MAURITIUS

South Tropic Line (Tropic of Capricorn)

AUSTRALIA

120°

| Below Sea Level | 100 m. 328 ft. | 200 m. 656 ft. | 500 m. 1,640 ft. | 1,000 m. 3,281 ft. | 2,000 m. 6,562 ft. | 5,000 m. 16,404 ft. |
|---|---|---|---|---|---|---|

80° Longitude East of Greenwich 100°

The ibex is a wild goat of the Himalayas

Marco Polo's sheep is largest of sheep family

rivers flow into the Persian Gulf. These rivers provide oases in a very dry region. In north China, the Hwang Ho, sometimes called the Yellow River, has built up a vast floodplain. This river actually lies above the level of the surrounding land. It is held in place by both natural and man-made levees. When great floods occurred in the past, many lives were lost from drowning or from the famines which followed. The Yangtze and the Si are two important drainage systems in China. The Irrawaddy and Mekong rivers are found in southeastern Asia.

In the north, there are many rivers flowing toward the Arctic Ocean. Three of the more important ones are the Lena, the Ob, and the Yensei. These rivers thaw, their mouths being the last to do so. This makes swampy and flooded conditions in the short summer season.

In central Asia there are many rivers which have no outlet to the sea. This vast region lacks a proper natural drainage system. As a result, these rivers flow into lakes and inland seas which are salty, such as the Aral and the Caspian seas.

The rainy season starts in the spring when steady moisture-laden winds blow from the Indian Ocean over the land. Differences in air pressure cause this constant movement. In the dry season, cold air over the continent exerts high pressure compared to the air over the Indian Ocean. For months the dry winds blow from land to water.

Most of China has a humid *subtropical* climate similar to that of southeastern United States. Rainfall is adequate and sufficient to support a forest cover. Southwestern Asia and much of the interior of the continent are very dry. Here the *tropical* deserts of Arabia and the Thar in northwest India are found. One desert, the Gobi of Mongolia, is too far from the equator to be a tropical desert. North of the Himalaya Mountains, the wind directions are generally west to east. The air is dry because it has blown over thousands of miles of land without the influence of bodies of water. The climate across Siberia is a *continental* type of climate with sufficient rain for a heavy forest cover known as the *taiga*. There are three to five frost-free months during a year.

### RIVERS AND DRAINAGE

Asia has many rivers. Those in southern and eastern Asia are very important to the people who live along their floodplains. The fertile plains where water is available for irrigation provide food for millions of people. The important rivers of India and Pakistan are the Ganges, the Brahmaputra, and the Indus. The Brahmaputra flows into the Ganges as it empties into the Bay of Bengal. In Iraq the Tigris and Euphrates

### PLANTS AND ANIMALS

Asia has a varied plant and animal life. In Siberia the land varies from TUNDRA in the north to steppes or prairie land in the central region and evergreen forests in the southeast. In the west, on the slopes of the Ural Mountains, forests of valuable HARDWOODS and conifers grow. The animal life in these varied habitats include the ermine, sable, bear, wolf, fox, marten, lynx, squirrel, skunk, otter, and hare.

Southwest Asia presents a contrast of dry lowlands and forested mountains. These forests are made up of oak, pine, fir, cypress, and cedars of Lebanon. In the valleys FRUIT trees like orange, apricot, cherry, plum, and fig grow abundantly, as do grapes and dates. Wild animals are still abundant in the mountains and include wolf,

**The giant panda of western China and Tibet was considered to be a myth until 100 years ago**

brown bear, leopard, tiger, mountain sheep, and deer. In the valleys and upland meadows sheep, goats, and camels are herded. Two varieties are unique—the angora (long-haired) goat of Turkey and the fat-tailed sheep of Afghanistan.

The high mountains of central Asia have great evergreen forests and animal life which includes mountain sheep and goats, musk deer, and the yak.

The monsoon regions of India and southeast Asia have three principal types of vegetation—savanna, tropical jungle, and mountain forests. The commercial trees include ebony, teak, sandalwood, and bamboo—a tree-like grass. Jute, for making burlap bags, and spices, like pepper, tumeric, ginger, and anise, are gathered from wild plants or are cultivated. Cinnamon bark, rubber, and coconuts are harvested from native and cultivated trees.

The wild animals of India, Myanmar (Burma), and southeast Asia include the tiger, leopard, elephant, monkey, honey bear, water buffalo, and wild dogs. The elephant and water buffalo are domesticated for heavy work.

The plant and animal life of China has all the variations of Asia as a whole, from the cold forested mountains of Manchuria to the tropical jungles of southeast Asia, and from the monsoon east to the deserts and mountains of the west.

## NATURAL RESOURCES

The economic value of Asia's mineral resources, especially PETROLEUM, is almost unimaginable. The U.S. Congress Research Service estimates that before oil began to be consumed by humans, the world contained around 2,215 billion barrels of usable petroleum. By 1992, nearly one-third had been used. Of the earth's remaining oil, more than three-fourths is in Asia. Middle Eastern nations touching the Persian Gulf have about one-half of the planet's known petroleum reserves. Nations of the former Soviet Union and, to a lesser extent, China and Indonesia, also have sizeable reserves.

Asia has vast amounts of natural GAS and COAL. Geologists estimate that sixty percent of the world's remaining coal is found within the borders of the former Soviet Union, which has recently been the world's largest producer of natural gas. The Persian Gulf area is even richer in natural gas reserves. Significant coal deposits are found throughout China and in parts of Korea and India.

Huge deposits of IRON ore are found in the former Soviet Union and in China. MANGANESE, used to make steel, is also plentiful in the same areas and India as well. Malaysia and Indonesia have vast TIN reserves. Other minerals found in Asia include BAUXITE (used in making aluminum), manganese from India and China, precious jewels, CHROMIUM, TUNGSTEN, ZINC, and more.     P.P.S./D.H.J./J.H.

**Asp** see Snakes

**Asparagus** (as-PAIR-uh-gus) The new young shoots of this plant are eaten as a vegetable. It has no true leaves. The fruit is a small red berry.

The roots of asparagus plants grown from seed are set in a ridge of soil. As the asparagus grows, the trenches are filled.

When the stems are 6 inches (15.24 centimeters) or longer, they are cut below the ground. Three to five stalks on each root are left to develop into stems and leaves.

Asparagus has a fibrous perennial ROOT system which sends up shoots or spears for 15 to 20 years. The scales on the stem are modified branches. If the plant is permitted to grow, it becomes woody and bushy. The small flowers are greenish-yellow and drooping. The stamens and pistils are on different plants.

Asparagus is low in food value, having some protein and 94 per cent water. It is a member of the family Liliaceae.     H. J. C.

**Aspen** It is a type of poplar tree. The simple leaves have saw-toothed edges. The FLOWERS and fruits form long catkins. The seed pod is light green.

The leaves of aspens are alternately arranged on the stem. The sexes are separate, having male and female flowers on different trees. They are members of the family Salicaceae.

The bigtooth aspen has soft, light, close-grained wood. It grows from 30 to 50 feet (9.14 to 15.24 meters) high. The quaking aspen grows from 20 to 40 feet (6.1 to 12.19 meters) tall. Its wood is brittle, soft, and weak.     H.J.C.

SEE ALSO: ANGIOSPERM, POPLAR

**Large-toothed aspen**

**Asphalt** Asphalt is obtained from the materials left from petroleum refining. It also occurs naturally as asphaltum, a brown to black pitchlike substance. It is used for roads and for waterproofing.

The characteristics of asphalt account for its many uses. By comparison to other building materials used for the same purpose, it is cheaper and usually easier to work.

Asphalt was used in ancient times to make ships and reservoirs watertight. Stone walls were held together with it and roads were made smooth and durable. Asphalt, commonly called *pitch,* is organic in origin. It is found in pools or lakes which were formed by the

Asphalt is a common substance for road surfaces

remains of ancient plants and animals. Some of the best deposits in the Western Hemisphere are in Trinidad and Venezuela. It is also found in scattered areas of Europe and the Far East.

Useful supplies of asphalt are found in some porous rock formations, but most of the asphalt used today is obtained synthetically as the thick residue of processed PETROLEUM. In its natural state or its processed form, it is black or dark brown in color. It may flow like thick syrup or be as hard as a rock.

Because of its many uses, asphalt has great commercial value. It can withstand great variations in heat and is quite flexible. It mixes well with crushed rock or other construction materials, and it can support great stresses without breaking.     D. E. Z.

**Asphyxia** (ass-FIX-ee-uh) Asphyxia is a condition in which the supply of oxygen in the body is too low and the supply of carbon dioxide is too great. For life, it is necessary that the BLOOD continuously take a fresh supply of oxygen to the cells and receive carbon dioxide from them as waste materials. In CARBON MONOXIDE poisoning, caused by smoke, automobile exhaust, or gas fumes, there is breathing interference with this process. Carbon monoxide has a much greater attraction for the hemoglobin of the blood than does oxygen. If there is carbon monoxide in the lungs, the hemoglobin reacts with it rather than with oxygen. This lack of oxygen may result in death of the cells.

In cyanide poisoning, the blood carries its usual oxygen supply to the cells but the enzymes of the cells are affected so as to make the exchange of oxygen and carbon dioxide impossible.

Mountain climbers often suffer with asphyxia. At very high altitudes the air has a low oxygen content.

In such accidents as drownings, chokings, hangings or any other blockage of the air passages, there is interference in the process of inhalation and expiration.

Newborn babies may also experience asphyxia when their lungs fail to expand fully at birth. G. A. D.

SEE ALSO: RESPIRATORY SYSTEM

**Asphyxiation** see Asphyxia, First aid

**Aspirin** Aspirin is a white crystalline compound. It is the *ester* of salicylic acid and ACETIC ACID —*acetylsalicylic acid.* Proper dosage tends to reduce the body temperature of a person with a fever. It relieves certain types of joint and muscular pains and is used for colds and fever. Aspirin (in larger dosage) has been effective in treating symptoms of acute RHEUMATIC FEVER, and arthritis.

The name aspirin is derived from the early name for salicylic acid which was known as *Acidum Spiricum.*

Acetylsalicylic acid was prepared first by Gerhardt in 1853 and then by Kraut in 1869, by the action of acetyl chloride upon sodium salicylate (a salt of salicylic acid). A United States patent was issued to Hoff-

man in 1900 for its preparation by the action of acetic anhydride on salicylic acid. This formula was considered to have different chemical and medical properties from any American fever drug previously patented. It was at this time that aspirin was introduced for commercial use. W. J. K.

SEE ALSO: DRUGS, ESTER

**Assaying** (uh-SAY-ing) Assaying is a process used to find out how much and what kinds of metals are in a rock sample or an unknown mineral ore. The main methods of assaying are the *wet process* and the *fire process.*

In wet assaying, the unknown sample is mixed with other chemicals of known concentration, and the resulting products are then weighed.

In the fire process, the sample is first crushed and the pure substances removed. The sample is then heated until all impurities are burned off, leaving only the metal to be collected and weighed. P.P.S.

SEE ALSO: METAL, MINERAL

**Assimilation** The body must have food to remain alive and healthy. But many foods cannot be used in the form in which they are taken into the body. They must first be changed by *digestion* into simple units. These units can then be used as building blocks for larger, more complicated substances needed by the body in its *protoplasm.* Assimilation is the incorporation of the end products of digestion into living protoplasm within the cells of the body.

Foods belong to three basic groups: carbohydrates, fats and proteins. For assimilation into living protoplasm, carbohydrates must be changed into simple SUGARS; fats into FATTY ACIDS and glycerol; proteins into AMINO ACIDS. These basic building blocks can then be used as needed to put together the protoplasm required by the body. Water, minerals, and enzymes are also necessary in the process of assimilation. G. A. D.

SEE ALSO: ABSORPTION, DIGESTIVE SYSTEM, METABOLISM

**Astatine** (ASS-ta-teen) Astatine was the second man-made element. It decays quickly. (In Greek astatine means "unstable.") The symbol for astatine is At. Its atomic number is 85.

Astatine was first prepared by D.R. Corson, K.R. MacKenzie, and E. Segre at the University of California in 1940. Astatine-211 was prepared by bombarding bismuth-209 with an alpha particle. A cyclotron gave the alpha particle enough energy to react with bismuth. The world probably has no more than 30 grams of astatine. Astatine has 21 isotopes with atomic masses ranging from 200 to 219 ½ lives ranging from 8.3 hours to a fraction of a second. Chemically, astatine reacts like iodine.            A.J.H.

SEE ALSO: ELEMENT, CHEMICAL

**Aster** *Aster* means *star,* and the flower head of the aster plant looks like one. It is a composite plant and instead of one big flower has many tiny flowers in a cluster. The flower head may measure ½ to 6 inches (1.3 to 15.2 centimeters) across. Asters bloom in the fall.

The *annual* or *China aster* was once a tiny flower, but the modern hybrids are large and showy. They come in every color except yellow. The plant grows 1 to 3 feet (.3-.9 meters) tall with a thin stem, many leaves near the ground, and a giant flower head.

The *Stokes aster* is a wild perennial. The long leaves grow from a hairy stem. The blossoms are purple to blue.

The perennial *hardy asters* were developed by crossing the Italian, New York, and New England varieties. They grow 10 to 70 inches (25.4-177.8 cen-

**Aster** Courtesy Society For Visual Education, Inc.

timeters) high. The *yellow aster,* a perennial of eastern states, is not grown widely. It thrives in poor soil.                    H.J.C.

SEE ALSO: COMPOSITE FLOWER

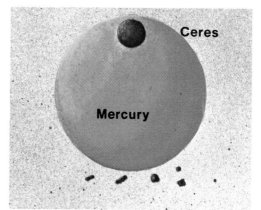

Ceres, the largest asteroid, is 490 miles (789 kilometers) in diameter. It is only 1/6 the size of our smallest planet, Mercury, which has a diameter of 3009 miles (4843 kilometers). Some asteroids, like those pictured below Mercury, are small and irregularly shaped.

**Asteroid** (ASS-ter-royd) Asteroid means "like a star." Planetoid means "like a planet." Asteroids, also called planetoids, are heavenly bodies that look something like stars. Actually, they are minor PLANETS. They are much, much smaller than the planets of the SOLAR SYSTEM. Some of them are only 1 mile (1.61 kilometers) in diameter.

The largest asteroid known is *Ceres.* It has a diameter of about 490 miles (788.6 kilometers). *Vesta* is the brightest one and is the only one that can be seen without a telescope.

"Bode's Law", a mathematical relationship developed by Johann Titus and presented by Johann Bode, predicted a planet between Mars and Jupiter. Bode suggested that searching in this area would lead to its discovery. On January 1, 1801, Guiseppi Piazzi found a new star while comparing his observations and star charts. The next night Piazzi checked his observations and found the new star had moved. He concluded that he had discovered a new planet. Bode felt that this was his predicted planet. The planet was actually the asteroid Ceres. C.L.K.

SEE ALSO: ORBIT, STAR

**Asthma** Asthma is a disease that affects breathing. A person with asthma cannot breathe normally. A person who has played so hard that he or she is out of breath and has to rest in order to catch their breath is going through what a person with asthma goes through. The asthmatic person is breathless because he or she is sick.

The part of the body involved in an attack of asthma is the LUNGS Within the chest are two lungs that fill with air whenever a person takes a breath. Leading to the lungs from the throat is the *trachea* or windpipe. The trachea branches out to each lung, both to the right and to the left, through smaller tubes called *bronchial tubes.*

During an attack of asthma, the bronchial tubes swell, and the air passageway through the tubes becomes so small that air is almost cut off from the lungs. An attack of asthma may come when the asthmatic person breathes dust from plants (POLLEN), household dust, animal fur, feathers, flour, or face powder. The same thing may happen when the person eats certain foods such as milk, eggs, or wheat. When these particles and foods are taken into the body, they may cause an allergic reaction with the release of histamine. Histamine stimulates swelling of the tissues and increased secretions. This, plus the spasm and narrowing by the smooth muscles in the bronchial walls, severely restricts the amount of air flow, causing wheezing.

Nervousness and emotional disturbance sometimes account for an attack of asthma. If a person is very tired from overwork and he then experiences an emotional upheaval (the death of a loved one or becoming very angry) he may develop an asthmatic attack.

During an asthmatic attack the victim's breathing out is long and "wheezy" while his breathing in is labored and difficult. He sits with his elbows on his knees and his head down in order to get help from every muscle of his back and shoulders in his struggle for air. Attacks may last for days or even weeks. Activity or breathing cold air, dust, or fumes, tend to worsen the attack. The patient may have to sleep sitting up, catching "cat naps" between periods of distress. He will probably awaken several times during the night to wheeze and cough until relief comes from some form of medication.

Many medicines bring relief to the asthmatic patient. ADRENALIN and ephedrine relax the bronchial muscle constriction. Antihistamines are of limited use despite the allergic component of much asthma, because they are very drying and cause secretions to thicken. However, Aminophylline and its derivatives are very useful in preventing or decreasing spasm. Inhaled CORTISONE, and, if necessary, cortisone given by vein or mouth, removes symptoms of stress and inflammation. Prevention is sometimes possible by avoiding or hyposensitizing to allergens, providing a dust-free and respiratory infection-free environment; by giving Aminophylline before attacks might occur; and by taking Cromolyn Sodium (a new drug) daily.

E.S.S./D.C.H.

SEE ALSO: ALLERGY, RESPIRATORY SYSTEM

**Astigmatism** (uh-STIGG-muh-tizz-uhm) An astigmatism is a visual defect. A person with an astigmatism is unable to see objects clearly. Images appear blurred, fuzzy and often elongated. To see images clearly the rays of light coming into the eye must focus directly on the retina. In astigmatism rays of light from an object pass through the structures of the EYE and focus in different planes. Some focus in front of the retina; some focus on the retina; some focus behind the retina. This difficulty in focusing is caused by defects in the curvature of the lens or cornea.

In some cases of astigmatism defects in curvature are caused by disease or injury. This form of astigmatism is rare and can be corrected by treating the disease or the injury which causes it.

The most common form of astigmatism is present from birth and is due to an abnormal structure of the eye. Astigmatism can be corrected through lenses (eyeglasses) which are ground so as to redirect the light rays which are out of focus.

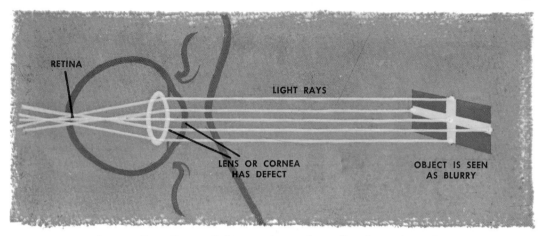

In an astigmatic eye, light rays do not focus directly on the retina

Persons suffering from astigmatism may very occasionally experience other difficulties besides poor vision. Some of the other symptoms are headaches and drowsiness (especially when the eyes are used for a longer period of time).            G. A. D.

SEE ALSO: FARSIGHTEDNESS, NEARSIGHTEDNESS, OPTOMETRY

**Astragalus** The astragalus is a BONE of the foot called the *ankle bone* in man.

SEE: SKELETON

**Astringent** (uh-STRIN-jent) An astringent is a substance that draws together living tissues. It is used in medicine as a drug to cause contracting or binding of wounds and to stop the escape of fluids from living cells.

Astringents may act to stop bleeding from wounds by constricting the capillary blood vessels. They may also prevent DIARRHEA or shrink the nasal or urinary passages when INFLAMMATION swells the mucous membranes. The discharges are stopped and the tissues can heal more easily.

Some substances that act as astringents are alum, tannin, silver nitrate, zinc sulfate, and dilute mineral acids.            B. B. G.

**Astrolabe** The astrolabe was an instrument used by sailors before the sextant was invented. Latitude could be determined by measuring the altitude of heavenly bodies.            H. S. G.

SEE ALSO: ASTRONOMY, NAVIGATION

**Astrology** (ah-STRAHL-oh-jee) Almost from the beginning of history men have believed that stars and constellations influence events on Earth. They felt that those who studied the stars could predict coming events. This study was called *astrology*.

In early times, astrologers knew more about the heavens than anyone else. Later, scientists began to separate true facts from superstitions. This study was called *astronomy*. Astrology has now been replaced by scientific astronomy and is not now considered to be a real science.

Astrology began in the ancient Biblical lands of the Near East. It developed there and in many other early lands, especially in India. The ability of ancient astrologers with limited knowledge and crude instruments was truly remarkable. They gave man his first real knowledge of the universe. They discovered many important facts about the space beyond Earth, how to predict eclipses, movement of stars, planets and groups of stars. But it was difficult for them to distinguish true facts from mere beliefs. Even today many people believe their lives are influenced by the stars and planets.

Today, newspapers often print predictions called horoscopes. These are based on birthdates that fall under the different signs of the zodiac. However, there are no scientific bases for the predictions.            J. A. C.

SEE ALSO: SUPERSTITIONS, ZODIAC

**Astronaut** (ASS-troh-not) An astronaut is a man or woman who has been trained to fly in space. These persons are carefully selected and undergo several years of training. Special astronaut wings are awarded to pilots who have flown at least 50 miles (80.47 kilometers) above the earth.

Many of today's astronauts are not rated pilots, but are experts in other scientific disciplines—geologists, astronomers, meteorologists, and physicists, for example. These astronauts go into space as passengers on the Space Shuttle missions to perform scientific experiments.

Among the missions they will perform are: global crop production forecasting; timber inventory and rangeland assessment; large-scale weather forecasting; earthquake prediction; solar power relay via satellites; international and domestic communications; basic physics and chemistry studies; ocean dynamics; and studies of the earth's ionosphere-magnetosphere coupling.

The first astronauts were selected on the basis of their experience in flying jets and their training in engineering. In the mid-1960s NASA began to stress academic excellence over actual flight experience and then provided needed flight training.

The training programs established for early manned flights such as *Apollo* and *Skylab* were rigorous. Complex simulators duplicated emergency situations in space; giant centrifuges helped astronauts experience up to seven Gs (seven times the force of gravity); special jet maneuvers exposed astronauts to weightlessness. Even landings on the moon were simulated.

"There's a half earth tonight." This is the Earth as it appeared to Apollo 8 crew members as they orbited the moon on Christmas Eve.

NASA

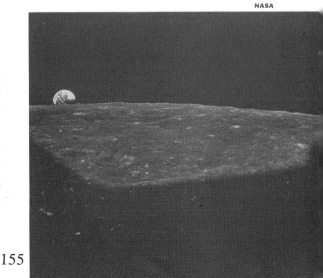

| DATES | SPACECRAFT | ASTRONAUTS |
|---|---|---|
| **1961** (May 5; Jul. 21) | *Mercury 3; 4* | Alan Shepard; Gus Grissom |
| **1962** (Feb. 20; May 24; Oct. 3) | *Mercury 6; 7; 8* | John Glenn; Scott Carpenter; Wally Schirra |
| **1963** (May 15-16) | *Mercury 9* | Gordon Cooper |
| **1965** (Mar. 23; Jun. 3-7; Aug. 21-29; Dec. 4-18/15-16) | *Gemini 3; 4; 5; 6/7* | G. Grissom, John Young; Ed White, Jim McDivitt; G. Cooper, Pete Conrad; Frank Borman, Jim Lovell/W. Schirra, Tom Stafford |
| **1968** (Oct. 11-22; Dec. 21-27) | *Apollo 7; 8* | W. Schirra, Walter Cunningham, Don Eisele; F. Borman, J. Lovell, Bill Anders |
| **1969** (Mar. 3-13; May 18-26; Jul. 16-24; Nov. 14-24) | *Apollo 9; 10; 11; 12* | Red Schweickart, J. McDivitt, David Scott; T. Stafford, J. Young, Gene Cernan; Neil Armstrong, Mike Collins, Edwin "Buzz" Aldrin; Charles Conrad, Dick Gordon, Alan Bean |
| **1970** (Apr. 11-17) | *Apollo 13* | J. Lovell, Fred Haise, John Swigert, Jr. |
| **1971** (Jan. 31-Feb. 9; Jul. 26-Aug. 7) | *Apollo 14; 15* | A. Shepard, Stuart Roosa, Edgar Mitchell; Alfred Worden, D. Scott, James Irwin |
| **1972** (Apr. 16-27; Dec. 7-19) | *Apollo 16; 17* | Charles Duke, Jr., Thomas Mattingly; G. Cernan, Ronald Evans, Harrison Schmitt |
| **1973** (May 14-Jun. 22; Jul. 28-Sep. 25) | *Skylab 2; 3* | C. Conrad, Joseph Kerwin, Paul Weitz; A. Bean, Owen Garriott, Jack Lousma |
| **1974** (Nov. 16-Feb. 8) | *Skylab 4* | Gerald Carr, Edward Gibson, William Pogue |
| **1975** (Jul. 15-24) | *Apollo 18-Soyuz* | Vance Brand, T. Stafford, Donald Slayton *(1st joint international flight)* |
| **SPACE SHUTTLES** | | |
| **1981** (Apr. 12-14; Nov. 12-14) | *Columbia* | Robert Crippen, J. Young; Joe Engle, Richard Truly |
| **1982** (Mar. 22-30; Jun. 27-Jul. 4; Nov. 11-16) | *Columbia* | J. Lousma, C. Gordon Fullerton; T. Mattingly, Henry Hartsfield, Jr.; V. Brand, Robert Overmyer, William Lenoir, Joseph Allen |
| **1983** (Apr. 4-9; Jun. 6-24; Aug. 30-Sep. 5) | *Challenger* | P. Weitz, Karol Bobko, Story Musgrave, Donald Peterson; Robert Crippen, Norman Thagard, John Favian, Frederick Hauck, Sally Ride *(1st U.S. woman in space)*; R. Truly, Daniel Brandenstein, William Thornton, Guion Bluford *(1st U.S. black in space)*, Dale Gardner |
| (Nov. 28-Dec. 8) | *Columbia* | J. Young, Brewster Shaw, Jr., Robert Parker, O. Garriott, Bryon Lichtenbert, Ulf Merbold |
| **1984** (Feb. 3-11; Apr. 6-13) | *Challenger* | V. Brand, Robert Gibson, Ronald McNair, Bruce McCandless, Robert Stewart; R. Crippen, Francis Scobee, George Nelson, Terry Hart, James Van Hoften |
| (Aug. 30-Sep. 5) | *Discovery* | Charles Walker, H. Hartsfield, Michael Coates, Judy Resnick, Steven Hawley, Richard Mullaine |
| **1985** (Jan. 25-28) | *Discovery* | T. Mattingly, Loren Shriver, James Buchli, Ellison Onizuka, Gary Payton |
| **1986** (Jan. 28) | *Challenger* | Christa McAuliffe *(1st citizen observer in space)*, F. Scobee, Michael J. Smith, J. Resnick, Ronald McNair, Gregory Jarvis, E. Onizuka *(all killed in explosion at launch)* |
| **1988** (Sep. 29-Oct. 3) | *Discovery* | F. Hauck, Richard Covey, David Hilmers, G. Nelson; John Lounge |
| **1990** (Nov. 15-20) | *Atlantis* | R. Covey, F. Culbertson, Robert Springer, Carl Meade, Chas. Gemar |
| **1992** (Sep. 12-20) | *Endeavour* | R. Gibson, Curtis Brown, Mark Lee, Mamoru Mohri *(1st Japanese U.S. citizen)*, Jay Apt, Jan Davis, Mae Jemison *(1st U.S. black woman in space)* |

When NASA needed astronauts for the Space Shuttle program, they wanted two kinds—pilots and mission specialists. Pilots had to pass a tough flight physical test and have at least a bachelor's degree in either engineering, biological or physical science, or mathematics. Mission specialists had to have at least a bachelor's degree in one of the same fields as the pilots, plus three years of related work in their fields.

On the Space Shuttle, payload specialists are also allowed to fly on missions. These nonastronauts are people who have worked on various payloads, such as satellites, to be carried on the shuttle or people who will perform experiments in the Spacelab. They get most of their training from the the organizations that send up the payloads, but NASA gives them courses in how to live in space and in emergency procedures.

Space Shuttle astronuats are much more broadly trained than were the early astronauts. They are required to know more about their spacecraft, to have a broader education in science, and to be able to double for ill or injured fellow crew members.

SEE ALSO: ASTRONAUTICS, COSMONAUT, SPACE, SPACE MEDICINE, SPACE TRAVEL

**Astronautics** (ass-troh-NAW-ticks)
Astronautics is the art and science of
space flight. Space is that vast expanse
beyond the blanket of air that surrounds our planet, the earth. Space
will not support life as we know it.
Therefore, it is necessary to take our
atmosphere with us if we are to travel
in this hostile realm.

*Astronautics* is closely related to
AERONAUTICS.. The craft, instruments,
and training of pilots for very high
altitude flight are similar to many of
the needs of astronautics. The term
AEROSPACE is frequently used to describe the combined fields of activity.

The National Aeronautics and
Space Administration was established
by an act of Congress in 1958 to
advance the peaceful exploration of
space for the benefit of mankind.

Advances in aeronautics and many
of the other scientific fields have made
space flight possible *only* within the
past 30 years. Powerful rockets are
necessary to overcome the pull of the
earth's gravity. Once beyond the
earth's atmosphere, spacecraft must
be placed into orbit at speeds of about
17,500 miles (28,163.5 kilometers)
per hour. The first satellite, called
SPUTNIK I, was placed in orbit by Russia
on October 4, 1957. The United States
launched *Explorer I* as its first satellite
on January 31, 1958.

By 1977 more than 2,000 craft had
been launched. Astronauts and cosmonauts have flown approximately
33,120 man-hours in space. Each flight
adds to the knowledge and skills of
space flight.

Many spacecraft work for us every
day. Good examples are the weather,
communications and navigation

Jet Propulsion Laboratory

Before any space launch the Saturn V is thoroughly
checked to prevent mechanical failure in flight.

satellites. These craft are constantly
sending back new knowledge about
our earth, the solar system, and the
universe.

Among the fascinating newer satellites
planned or now flying are:

A *Geostationary Meteorological Satellite*
(GMS) developed by Hughes Aircraft
Company for Japan to keep a weather eye
on typhoons, hurricanes, monsoons, and
other western Pacific storms.

*Marisat,* the world's first Maritime
Satellite System, now in orbit over both the
Atlantic and Pacific oceans, to replace
Morse Code messages with high-quality
voice, telex, facsimile, and other data
transmission.

*VAS (Visible Infrared Spin-Scan
Radiometer Atmospheric Sounder),* which
was launched in 1980, is returning a three-
dimensional picture of Earth's cloud cover
to improve long-range weather forecasting.

*ATS-1,* which has been in orbit for a
decade, still performs missions of mercy for
sick and injured persons in remote areas of

Alaska, relaying medical instructions for treatment.

Two *Pioneer Venus* spacecraft, launched in 1978, compared the weather on Venus to the weather on Earth.

*Viking 1* and *2,* which flew by Jupiter and Saturn, returned stunning pictures and much information about their atmospheres.

GENERAL PRINCIPLES OF
SPACECRAFT IN MOTION

Men have studied the universe for centuries. Our sun has been identified as a minor star in our galaxy with a family of nine planets. The nearest star, Proxima Centauri, is 4⅓ light years away. (Light travels 300,000 kilometers or 186,000 miles a sec-

ond.) The vastness of space and our universe is beyond comprehension, yet the movement of the heavenly bodies is orderly and predictable. The massive gravitational pull of our sun, which is 93,000,000 miles or 149,668,990 kilometers away, holds the planets in orbit. The earth has its own gravitational force which must be overcome and then balanced if man-made spacecraft are to be placed in orbit.

Johannes Kepler formulated three laws early in the seventeenth century which, along with Sir Isaac Newton's laws of gravity and motion, permits scientists to determine the motion of the planets and other celestial bodies. These laws may also be used to calculate the flight paths of satellites as well as other spacecraft which are being sent into space.

Any vehicle moving in space is subject to gravity. For a satellite to orbit, it is necessary to accelerate it to *orbital velocity.* This is the velocity at which the force of gravity is offset by speed. The orbital velocity varies with the distance above the earth as the gravitational pull decreases with altitude. A spacecraft 200 miles (321.9 kilometers) above the earth requires a velocity of about 17,500 miles (28,163.5 kilometers) per hour. At a distance equal to that of the moon (240,000 miles or 386,243 kilometers) an orbit would be achieved at a velocity of only 2,000 miles (3218.7 kilometers) per hour. Vehicles in space tend to maintain their speed of travel while coasting, since the near vacuum of space does not create resistance like the atmosphere.

To send a spacecraft to the moon or beyond, it is necessary to achieve a higher escape velocity. This speed also varies with altitude. At lower altitudes approximately 25,000 MPH (40,234 kilometers) is necessary to travel a path away from the earth. Escape velocity means that the craft will not fall back to earth.

Space is a hostile environment for man and his vehicles. Spacecraft must withstand the extremes of temperatures, radiation, and the almost complete vacuum found away from the earth's insulating atmosphere. The manned craft must also withstand the shock and heat of reentry to return safely.

The National Aeronautics and Space Administration (NASA) heads our space explora-

| PURPOSE | ORBIT DATE | NAME | ASSIGNMENT |
|---|---|---|---|
| Communication | Aug. 12, 1960 | Echo | Passive communication |
| Communication (Active) | Jul. 10, 1962 | Telstar I | Relay TV programs between U.S./Europe |
| | Apr. 6, 1965 | Early Bird | First commercial communications |
| | Jan. 11, 1976 | INTELSAT 2B | First in stationary orbit—TV, data |
| | Feb. 19, 1976 | Marisat | Maritime communications |
| | Feb. 21, 1981 | Comstar D | Part of worldwide system |
| | Jun. 15, 1988 | Pan American | First privately owned international satellite |
| Weather | Feb. 17, 1959 | Vanguard | First to return weather to earth |
| | Sep. 9, 1980 | GOES D | Storm tracking |
| | Dec. 12, 1984 | NOAA 5 | Worldwide search and rescue operations data |
| Navigation | Apr. 13, 1960 | TRANSIT | First navigation satellite |
| | Feb. 21, 1978 | Navstar | Provides continuous data on positions |
| Scientific | Jan. 31, 1958 | Explorer | First U.S. satellite |
| | Mar. 7, 1962 | OSO | Orbiting solar observatory |
| | Dec. 6, 1966 | ATS | Applications Technology test vehicle |
| | Dec. 2, 1968 | OAO | First orbiting astronomical observatory |
| | Jul. 23, 1972 | Landsat | Earth imaging |
| | Oct. 24, 1978 | Nimbus | Data on earth's atmosphere, oceans |
| | Feb. 14, 1980 | Solar Max | Study solar flares on sun and causes |
| | Nov. 18, 1989 | COBE | Map cosmic radiation |
| | Apr. 27, 1990 | Hubble Telescope | Detect ultraviolet/infrared rays from celestial objects |
| | Apr. 7, 1991 | Gamma Ray | Data on unusual objects as black holes |
| Military | May 9, 1963 | ICBM | Defense warning system |

tion efforts. The knowledge, skills, and efforts of hundreds of thousands of people in government, industry, and the academic world have been used. Astronautics blends almost all scientific and technological fields known to man.

In terms of time and distance, the initial goal of exploring our own solar system may seem awesome and border upon the impossible. However, recent technological advances are indeed encouraging.

## LAUNCH VEHICLES

The first requirement of space flight is a sufficiently powerful engine to overcome the earth's gravitational pull. It must also be able to operate without need for oxygen from the atmosphere. The obvious answer lies in the rocket engine and its great thrust. Dr. Robert Goddard laid much of the foundation for modern rocketry with his liquid-fuel rocket experiments. The Germans developed the V-2 missile during World War II. After the war, the United States experimented with captured V-2 rockets and produced several missiles which were adapted to space missions.

A wide variety of liquid- and solid-fueled launch vehicles have been used in space exploration. The earliest and smallest solid fuel rocket used was named *Scout.* The largest is the huge *Saturn V,* which develops about 7.5 million pounds of thrust (160 million horsepower) from five liquid-fuel engines. Solid-fuel rocket boosters (SRBs) are used in Space Shuttle launches. These SRBs, unlike the earlier rockets, are reusable. During a launch an external tank supplies liquid fuel to the engines and is cast off when the shuttle reaches orbit.

The limitations of large chemical rockets for long-range missions such as a Mars manned landing have been studied, and an advanced nuclear rocket propulsion system (NERVA) is now under development. This rocket will have a specific impulse twice that of a high-energy chemical system, which will give it a major performance advantage.

## SCIENTIFIC SATELLITES
## AND
## INTERPLANETARY SPACECRAFT

The continuing series of scientific satellites since Russia's *Sputnik I* have provided vast amounts of information about our planet, its near space environment, and the universe. For example, the first American satellite, *Explorer I,* confirmed the great *Van Allen Radiation Belts.*

Scientific satellites in effect are extending our observations beyond the protective shield of the earth's atmosphere, ionosphere, and magnetic shell to report back the true nature of the space environment and the forces which affect our lives on the earth's surface.

Technological advances, such as microelectronics and solid state circuitry, have made possible a wide range of complex satellites. The *orbiting observatories* (OAO — astronomical, OSO — solar, OGO — geophysical); Pegasus, with its huge panels to relay data on micrometeoroids; and the Biosatellites, with their living organisms experiments are all part of the space research programs. A series of *Applications Technology Satellites* (ATS) is designed to test advanced components and techniques for future spacecraft.

The category of satellites designed to utilize space for betterment of our daily lives is known as *Applications Satellites.* Their high vantage point of a hundred miles (160.93 kilometers) or more offers obvious advantages in viewing wide area weather patterns and relaying radio, television, and telephone communications.

*Echo 1* became the first applications satellite as it achieved orbit on August 12, 1960. The 100-foot (30.48 meter) diameter balloon permitted radio waves to be bounced from one point to another thousands of miles away. Much popular interest was created as the balloon could frequently be seen from the ground.

The more efficient active-repeater vehicles placed into a synchronous orbit have emerged as the basis for regular worldwide communications which commenced in 1967. This kind of satellite appears to hover over a fixed position on the earth.

The weather satellites have perhaps stimulated the greatest interest among the public. *Tiros, Nimbus,* and *NOAA* are providing daily photographs of the weather patterns around the world. The discovery and tracking of major storms have assisted the meteorologists in preparing more accurate forecasts. It has been estimated that accurate five-day forecasts would probably save between 2½ and 5½ billion dollars annually in the United States alone. Agriculture, the construction industry, and government operations, such as flood control, would benefit greatly. Weather research is beginning to reveal the nature of the continent-sized weather patterns that form and dissolve over the oceans and land masses. Infrared sensors are adding information about the heat being added to and lost from the earth and its atmosphere.

Closely allied to the weather satellites is the LANDSAT program, an extension of the earlier Earth Resources Technology Satellite (ERTS) program. LANDSAT spacecraft cameras and sensors monitor and scrutinize the earth's surface to gather information as to agricultural patterns, ocean currents, geological features, and even unknown archeological sites. Other important uses of satellites include the establishment of an accurate navigational system and classified military reconnaissance and communications objectives.

On April 25, 1990, the Hubble Space Telescope (HST) was placed in orbit about 380 miles (610 km) above the earth's surface. Soon afterward, it was learned that the HST's main mirror, nearly 95 inches (2.4 m) in diameter, was not focused properly. Repairs in space were scheduled for 1993.

## SPACE PROBES

Scientific speculation as to the nature of the other planets and the possibility of finding the existence of life forms has continued for centuries. Mars and Venus have been generally agreed upon as the most likely to support extraterrestrial life. *Mariner 2* and *4* along with the Russian *Venera 4,* reported back over 36 million miles (58 million kilometers) that Venus is a very hot planet (about 800° F or 427° C) with a very dense atmosphere (about 80 percent carbon dioxide).

In 1973, *Mariner 10* blasted off for a swing-by of planets Venus and Mercury, closer to the sun than planet Earth, while two other space travelers, *Pioneer 10* and *11,* headed for the outer rim of the solar system.

The *Pioneer* spacecraft safely crossed the rocky asteroid belt between the orbits of Mars and Jupiter, and roughly one year later skirted the dangerous reefs of the Jovian radiation belts, took pictures of the Great Red Spot on Jupiter's surface, and cruised past four of the planet's moons, Io, Europa, Ganymede, and Callisto.

## IMPORTANT U.S. SPACE PROBES

| SATELLITE | LAUNCH DATE | ASSIGNMENT |
|---|---|---|
| Mariner 4 | Nov. 28, 1964 | Explored Venus, photographed Mars, measured conditions in space. |
| Mariner 9 | May 30. 1971 | First probe to orbit Mars. |
| Pioneer 10 | Mar. 2, 1972 | Explored Jupiter, the Milky Way; first spacecraft to escape solar system. |
| Viking 1 | Aug. 20, 1975 | Landed on Mars; sent photos and data. |
| Voyager 2 | Aug. 20, 1977 | Flew past Jupiter in 1979, Saturn in 1981, Uranus in 1986, Neptune in 1989; sent back photos and information on planets' moons. |
| Magellan | May 4, 1989 | Used radar to map surface of Venus. |
| Galileo | Oct. 18, 1989 | To reach Jupiter in 1995; to photograph earth, moon, Venus. |
| Ulysses | Oct. 6, 1990 | To examine polar regions of the sun in 1994, 1995; launched by United States and European Space Agency. |
| Solar Max | Jun. 7, 1992 | Ultraviolet explorer to catalog sources of ultraviolet light for insight into temperature, chemical makeup, density of stars. |

Surveyor — Jet Propulsion Laboratory

Apollo 18

NASA

## IMPORTANT U.S. MOON PROBES

| VEHICLE | FIRST LAUNCH | ASSIGNMENT |
|---|---|---|
| Ranger | Aug. 23, 1961 | Obtain high resolution photos of lunar surface. |
| Surveyor | May 30, 1966 | Soft landing on lunar surface with scientific payloads including soil sampler. |
| Lunar Orbiter | Aug. 10, 1966 | Photograph lunar surface from low altitudes to determine location for manned moon landing. |
| Lunar Orbiter 2 | Nov. 6, 1966 | Impacted moon; returned 205 lunar frames. |
| Lunar Orbiter 3 | Feb. 4, 1967 | Impacted moon; returned 182 lunar frames. |
| Surveyor 3 | Apr. 17, 1967 | Landed on moon; soil sampler and photo experiments. |
| Surveyor 5 | Sep. 8, 1967 | Landed on moon; returned 19,000 photos; soil analysis data. |
| Surveyor 6 | Nov. 7, 1967 | Landed on moon; first rocket takeoff from moon. |
| Surveyor 7 | Jan. 7, 1968 | Landed on moon; last of Surveyor series. |

## EMPLOYMENT OF LAUNCH VEHICLES

| LAUNCH VEHICLE | ASSIGNMENTS |
|---|---|
| Scout | Small Explorer satellites; ISIS; ESRO; San Marco; geoprobes; reentry studies; TRANSIT; Navstar. |
| Delta and TAD | TIROS, TOS, ESSA weather satellites; communications satellites (Telstar, Echo, Syncom); larger scientific satellites as Explorers XII, XIV, XV, XVII, XXIX; Ariel; Orbiting Solar Observatories; Interplanetary Explorers; Pioneer; Early Bird; Solar Max; GOES; NOAA 5. |
| Thor-Agena and TAT | Scientific satellites such as Alouette; Orbiting Geophysical Observatories; applications satellites such as Advanced Echo communications satellite and Nimbus weather satellite; ICBM. |
| Atlas D | Project Mercury; reentry research. |
| Atlas-Agena | Unmanned lunar and interplanetary probes such as Ranger, Lunar Orbiter, and Mariner; Orbiting Astronomical Observatory; Project Gemini; Applications Technology Satellite. |
| Atlas-Centaur | Surveyor spacecraft for soft landing on moon; advance Mariner spacecraft for exploration of Mars and Venus; OAO. |
| Titan II | Project Gemini. |
| Saturn I | Project Apollo earth-orbital flights of boilerplate command/service modules; carried first astronauts to moon. |
| Saturn I B | Project Apollo earth-orbital flights of command/service; lunar excursion modules; orbital rendezvous rehearsals; orbited first U.S. space station—Skylab. |
| Saturn V | Project Apollo lunar exploration missions. |
| SRB (Solid Rocket Boosters) | For space shuttle orbital launches; can be used for more than one flight. |

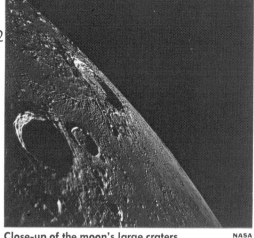

**Close-up of the moon's large craters**          NASA

Attached to *Pioneer 10* is a plaque depicting an Earth man and woman, diagrams of the solar system and pulsar radio frequencies, and other data in case some civilization beyond our solar system finds it and wants to know where it came from.

In July of 1976 *Viking I* landed on the planet Mars. It sent back pictures showing a rocky, sandy scene—much like a desert—with reddish soil. *Viking 2*'s lander touched down on Mars in August 1976 in a field of deeply pitted rocks that puzzled scientists.

*Voyager 1* and *2* passed by Jupiter in March and July of 1979. *Voyager 1* sent back pictures of Jupiter's main satellites, and *Voyager 2* showed scientists a heretofore unknown ring around the planet. When the two *Voyager* probes passed by Saturn a year and a half later, they showed that Saturn's rings were made up of many small ringlets, not broad bands. *Voyager 2* went on to explore Uranus and Neptune. In early 1986, it found ten new moons of Uranus. During two Space Shuttle missions in 1989, the *Magellan* probe was launched toward Venus, the *Galileo* probe toward Jupiter.

## LUNAR EXPLORATION

The landing of a man on the moon was set forth as a major objective of America's space exploration program. Several projects of unmanned and manned space flights were necessary to achieve the goal which was accomplished on July 20, 1969.

Project Ranger sent back the first close-up photographs of the moon. Features as small as 10 inches (25.4 centimeters) across were made visible to man for the first time. The 17,255 close-ups of the lunar surface provided the single greatest advance in lunar knowledge since Galileo first studied the moon through a telescope more than three centuries ago.

Another unmanned spacecraft called Lunar Orbiter photographed specific potential landing sites from a low lunar orbit. Some remarkable photographs, including a historic first look into the crater Copernicus, revealed evidence that there might be quakes and volcanic activity there.

The third lunar project, the Surveyor spacecraft series, soft landed on the moon and telecast thousands of close-up photographs. A device determined that the lunar soil probably has a consistency of wet sand.

Reliable radio communications and telecast information have answered many questions about the moon and space, but these were poor substitutes for manned exploration. Scientists began to design vehicles that could carry humans into space.

## MANNED SPACE FLIGHTS

The manned space flight program was started with the first Project Mercury astronaut being rocketed into space on May 5, 1961, following two-and-a-half years of rigorous training. Five additional flights proved that man could be placed in orbit, perform useful tasks, and return safely to earth.

The next step was Project Gemini. A two-man capsule was designed to be maneuvered into orbit to master the techniques of rendezvous and docking with another spacecraft. The 10 Gemini flights, which were concluded on November 15, 1966, proved man's ability to withstand the rigors of prolonged space flight. Also, experience was achieved in EVA (extra-vehicular activity). Extensive earth photographs were taken as part of the project's objectives.

The most ambitious and final stage of the NASA program, called Project Apollo, landed the first explorers on the moon July 20, 1969. A three-man command module, a service module equipped with rocket engine and fuel supplies, and a lunar module (LM) were mounted on top of the huge Saturn V rocket for launching. The three modules were flown together until the desired lunar orbit was achieved. Two astronauts separated the LM from the command module and flew the LM to the lunar surface for a several-hour period of exploration. The LM was then launched back into the orbit of the parent craft where the astronauts reboarded

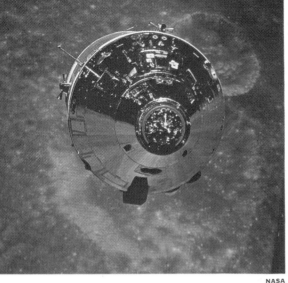

NASA

The Apollo Command Module carried three crew-
men. While two astronauts explored the lunar surface the pilot of the command module stayed in
orbit around the moon.

the command module. The service module
rocket boosted the parent craft out of the
lunar orbit and started the journey home.
The re-entry and landing with the command
capsule was similar to those experienced
with Mercury and Gemini. Thus ended the
greatest and most complex journey of
mankind.

### APOLLO

The first four manned Apollo missions to
test the spacecraft and flight techniques
were remarkably trouble free, including the
historic *Apollo 8* first flight into lunar orbit.
Astronaut Neil A. Armstrong was the
first man to set foot on the lunar surface
during the July, 1969 *Apollo 11* flight mission, followed by his co-pilot, Edwin
Aldrin. *Apollo 12* quickly followed with a
lunar landing on November 19, 1969, when
Astronauts Charles Conrad and Alan Bean
explored the lunar surface. Then, near-dis-
aster struck on April 13, 1970. An explosion
aboard *Apollo 13* in mid-trajectory crippled
the spacecraft. Millions of people on earth
followed the astronauts' dramatic 143-hour
ordeal on television before their craft safely
splashed down in the Pacific Ocean. Ships
from Russia, England, and France stood by
to help.
Astronauts Alan Shepard and Stuart A.
Mitchell of the *Apollo 14* crew spent 4¾
hours on the moon on February 5, 1971,
using a two-wheeled cart to travel over its
surface.
On July 30, 1971, *Apollo 15's* lunar
module Falcon landed in the Sea of Rains.

Astronauts David R. Scott and James B.
Irwin drove a lunar dune buggy 5 miles
(8.05 kilometers) to nearby St. George
crater and returned with a load of moon
rocks. One, called the Genesis rock, was
estimated to be 4.15 billion years old.
Astronaut John W. Young, commander
of *Apollo 16,* put the LRV (Lunar Roving
Vehicle) through a "Grand Prix" speed run
on the moon and hit 10.2 miles (16.4
kilometers) per hour. Later, he tripped over
a heat-flow experiment cable and tore it
loose accidentally. He and Charles M. Duke
Jr. made three other excursions in the LRV
before returning to earth.
Man's final scheduled trip to the moon
for this century was *Apollo 17,* launched
December 7, 1972, from Cape Kennedy.
Astronauts Eugene Cernan, Ronald Evans,
and Harrison Schmitt returned to splash-
down in the Pacific on December 19 with
249 pounds (113 kilograms) of lunar rocks,
some of them peculiarly orange and red,
indicating possible volcanism on the moon.
The 30th U.S. manned space flight, and
the 25th for Russian cosmonauts, took
place in mid-July, 1975, to join together in
space for the first time spacemen from two
nations. The Apollo 18-Soyuz Test Project
(ASTP) succeeded on July 17 at 11:15 A.M.
(CDT), with Russian and U.S. crews shak-
ing hands in space.

**Lunar Roving Vehicle (LRV)**          NASA

Rockwell International

The Space Shuttle differs from previous space vehicles in that it can be used again and again. Men and women, military personnel and civilian scientists, participate in the Space Shuttle's missions.

## ADVANCED MANNED SPACE PROGRAMS

On May 14, 1973, the U.S. moved into a new, advanced era of manned space flight when a large space station, *Skylab,* was launched from John F. Kennedy Space Center atop a *Saturn V* rocket into an earth orbit. A micrometeorite shield was ripped loose on takeoff.

Astronauts Charles Conrad, Joseph Kerwin, and Paul Weitz, launched from Cape Kennedy aboard an *Apollo* capsule, rendezvoused with *Skylab* on May 25, unstuck the shield, and worked 18 hours a day on scientific and engineering experiments. Their goal was to find out how man can live in space for extended periods. They returned to Earth on June 22, after nearly a month in orbit.

On July 28 three other astronauts spent 59 days aboard *Skylab*. They were replaced by another team of astronauts, who stayed 84 days. However, *Skylab* fell to Earth in 1981, ending this phase of space exploration. Scientists believe that the Earth's atmosphere expanded outward because of heavy solar activity, and *Skylab* experienced atmospheric drag that had not been anticipated, causing it to slow and eventually to fall out of orbit.

The world's first reusable space vehicle, the Space Shuttle, passed its initial tests beginning in 1977 and was launched into space on April 12, 1981. On its maiden flight the shuttle *Columbia* performed almost flawlessly.

After its safe return, *Columbia* was prepared for its next trip into space. Three more test flights were run; then the first operational flight of this "space truck" was undertaken on November 11, 1982. Two communications satellites were launched into orbit, and a number of experiments, including three proposed by students, were performed during the five-day mission.

Designed and built by Rockwell International, the NASA Space Shuttle can be launched over and over again, like an aircraft. The Space Shuttle crews deployed, repaired, and retrieved satellites.

After twenty-four successful Space Shuttle missions, tragedy struck on January 28, 1986, when the *Challenger* exploded during takeoff, killing the entire crew of seven astronauts. After the accident, the shuttle program was shut down for over two years while NASA corrected the problems that caused the explosion and overhauled the entire shuttle program. Launches resumed on September 29, 1988, with the successful mission of the shuttle *Discovery*.

Someday, perhaps, the shuttle will carry people to huge space colonies able to support thousands of inhabitants. They will go on voyages to distant planets in our vast Solar System. The colonies would be assembled in space from modules carried up by the shuttle. D.D

SEE ALSO: ASTRONAUT, COSMONAUT, ROCKETS, SPACE MEDICINE, SPACE TRAVEL, SPACE VEHICLES

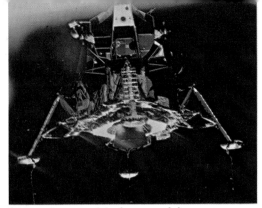

Above, close-up of the lunar module

Above, Aldrin walks toward the lunar module after setting up a solar wind experiment

Reflected in Aldrin's visor is Neil Armstrong, the first man to step on the moon.

Above, close-up of the moon's craters

Armstrong and Aldrin, first men on the moon, raise the American flag. Picture was taken automatically from the lunar module

Close-up of an astronaut's footprint on the moon's surface

(All, NASA)

Stars never before seen or analyzed are now being "discovered" by radio telescope

**Astronomy** The study of all of the heavenly bodies and the space that lies between them is the science of astronomy. Astronomy is one of the oldest true sciences. Throughout the ages men have gazed at the sky with interest and curiosity. The future of astronomy is exciting.

The earliest men on Earth saw the moon and the beautiful patterns of the stars at night. During the day they were aware of the large light in the SKY, the SUN, which is now known to be a necessity to life on Earth. They wondered what caused DAY AND NIGHT and what caused the regular changes of SEASONS. The very earliest practical application of the study of the skies was the making of CLOCKS and CAL-ENDARS to measure time. Early farmers needed a calendar to know when to plant their seeds so that their crops would survive. Because of their ability to predict the seasons, the men who studied the stars were considered very wise. People believed that they could predict and explain all kinds of happenings. The unscientific attempts to interpret man's past and predict his future by the stars is called ASTROL-OGY. Some people still believe in it.

The ancient concept of the universe seems very simple and limited today. Many years ago men believed that the earth was flat and that the sky was a large dome, or bowl, that fitted over the earth. The sun, the moon, and the stars were lamps that were hung inside the dome. The Greeks held the earth to be a sphere. Eudoxus (370 B.C.), a Greek mathematician, developed an earth-centered universe with the other celestial bodies on spheres moving around the earth. This model was built on by both Plato (428-348 B.C.) and Aristotle (384-322 B.C.). Aristotle's model of the universe was finally broken down by NICHOLAS COPERNICUS (1473-1543). In a book published just before his death, Copernicus made the sun the center of the solar system with the earth and other celestial bodies moving around the sun in circular orbits. Galileo later defended and built on the Copernican model.

Galileo Galilei (1564-1642) was the first astronomer to use a telescope for celestial observation. He first discovered the mountains on the moon. Then he found that the Milky Way was made up of millions of stars. His next and most important discovery was the four moons of Jupiter. He studied the sun and found that it was not perfect, but had blemishes.

Tyco Brahe (1546-1601) was the master of astronomical measurements. Brahe collected volumes of information about the stars and planets, but made little effort to interpret them. Johannes Kepler (1571-1630), an assistant to Brahe, used Brahe's records to determine the orbit of Mars to be elliptical with the sun at one of the centers of the ellipse. He also concluded that a line connecting the sun and a planet sweeps out equal areas in equal times. He found a relationship between a planet's from the sun and its period.

Sir Isaac Newton (1642-1727) presented a theory that all objects attract each other, "The Law of Universal Gravitational Attraction." He postulated that the interac-

The sun's corona is visible during a solar eclipse, which occurs when the moon passes between the earth and the sun.

tion between gravitational attraction and the "Law of Inertia" causes bodies to stay in orbital paths. The theory of relativity presented by Albert Einstein (1879-1955) refined further knowledge of the motions of celestial bodies.

Today it is known that the sun is just one of the billions of stars that are in the universe. There are nine known planets revolving around the sun: Mercury, Venus, Earth, Mars, Jupiter, Saturn, Uranus, Neptune, and Pluto. The sun and the planets that revolve around it are called a SOLAR SYSTEM. Future astronomers may discover that there are other solar systems, perhaps with life of some kind in them.

The earth rotates on its axis once every 24 hours. It makes a complete revolution around the sun in about 365¼ days. A body that revolves around another is called a SATELLITE. Earth and the other planets are satellites of the sun. The moon is a satellite of the earth.

The development of new techniques and new instruments is leading to a rapid accumulation of astronomical knowledge. Modern astronomers are aided in their research by new techniques that utilize many more areas of the spectrum than visible light. Instruments that gather information from the infrared, ultra-violet, X-ray, and gamma-ray areas of the spectrum have pushed back the frontiers of the universe.

Radio telescopes, first developed in the 1930s and 1940s, collect and amplify radio waves that are sent naturally from all parts of the universe. Recently, these devices have helped astronomers discover new types of starlike objects, called QUASARS and PULSARS, and learn more about matter scattered throughout the universe. In 1980, the Very Large Array (VLA) was completed in New Mexico. The VLA is made up of 27 separate radio telescopes that are electronically linked. A Very Long Baseline Array, linking a group of 10 radio telescopes spread across the United States, is scheduled for completion in the early to mid-1990s.

Optical telescopes, which use clear lenses and reflective mirrors to magnify faint light from distant objects, remain important tools of astronomy. In the 1990s, huge new optical telescopes are scheduled to be completed in Hawaii and northern Chile. Perhaps the most significant new telescope of all is the Hubble Space Telescope (HST), which was launched into earth orbit from the Space Shuttle *Discovery* on April 25, 1990. An orbiting telescope avoids virtually all the distortion created by the earth's atmosphere. Repairs on the HST, scheduled for 1993, were needed from the outset.

Breathtaking views of outer space come from the marriage of interplanetary rocket probes with digital electronic equipment. High-tech cameras, radio transmitters and receivers, and computerized imaging systems have produced highly detailed photos, even motion pictures, of many of our solar system's planets. Probes have even landed for extended tests on Mars (1976-1982) and Venus (1969, 1978, 1982). In the 1990s, Japan and the European Space Agency are also beginning the exploration of space.

A.J.H./J.H.

SEE ALSO: ASTRONAUTICS, EARTH, RADIO TELESCOPE, STAR; SATELLITE, MAN-MADE

**Astrophysics** ASTRONOMY developed centuries before *Astrophysics*. Today astronomy and astrophysics are considered the same. They use the latest methods of PHYSICS and CHEMISTRY to observe our UNIVERSE and its parts.

**Asymmetry** see Animals, classification of; Protozoa

**Atavism** Atavism is the reappearance in a living being of characteristics which have not been in its ancestors for several generations.
SEE: HEREDITY

**Athlete's Foot** Athlete's foot is a fungus infection of the toes and feet spread by moist conditions such as those found in locker room or swimming pool areas.

*Tinea Pedis* is the name of the particular type of ringworm fungus that infects the feet. It causes scaling, itching, blisters, and cracks between the toes and on the soles of the feet.

Treatment with "antifungal" lotions is usally effective. The condition can easily reoccur if the feet are not kept as dry as possible.                                   E.S.S.

**Atlantic Ocean** see Oceanography

**Atlas** see Rocket

**Atmosphere** (AT-muss-fere) The gaseous blanket of air that surrounds the earth is called the earth's atmosphere. It is like an ocean of air with man living at the bottom of the ocean. The atmosphere is always moving and the conditions in the atmosphere are always changing, from day to day and year to year.

COMPOSITION

The atmosphere is a mixture of odorless, colorless, and invisible gases. In addition to these gases, the atmosphere also contains water vapor (water in its gaseous form) and many different kinds of dust.

Much has been discovered about the atmosphere in recent times. As man has been able to travel in and through the atmosphere he has gained much new knowledge. The air has four important properties that help and protect man: (1) it protects the earth from extremes of heat and cold; (2) it is the source of oxygen for man; (3) it protects man from dangerous radiation that comes from the sun; and (4) it holds moisture.

| CONSTANT COMPONENTS OF THE ATMOSPHERE | | |
|---|---|---|
| Nitrogen | $N_2$ | 78.084% |
| Oxygen | $O_2$ | 20.946% |
| Argon | A | 0.934% |
| Carbon Dioxide | $CO_2$ | 0.033% |
| Neon | Ne | 0.00001818% |
| Helium | He | 0.00000524% |
| Methane | $CH_4$ | 0.000002% |
| Krypton | Kr | 0.00000114% |
| Hydrogen | $H_2$ | 0.0000005% |
| Nitrous Oxide | $N_2O$ | 0.0000005% |
| Xenon | Xe | 0.000000087% |

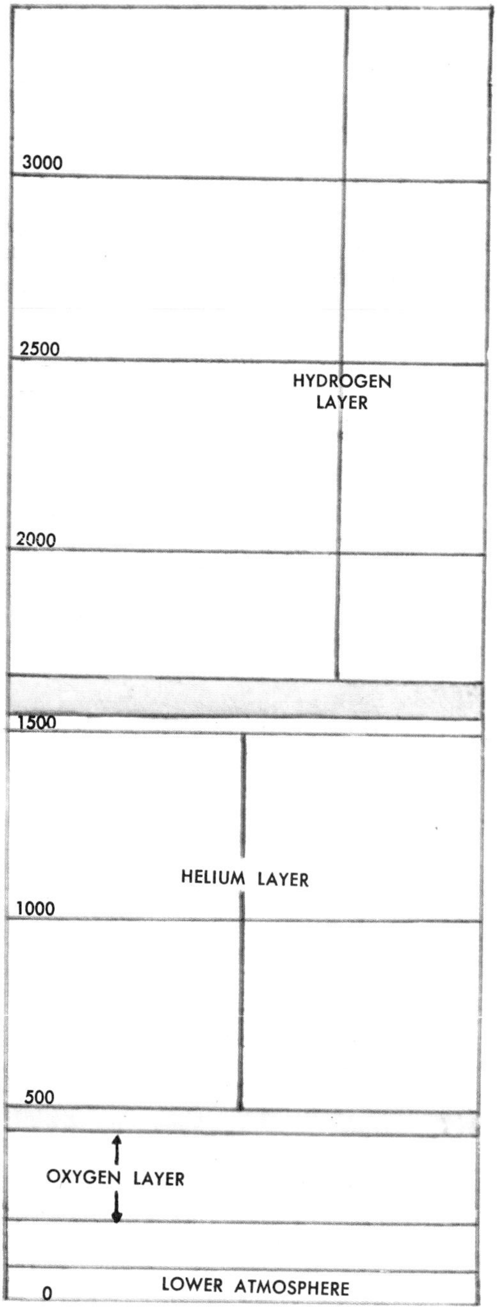

3000

2500

HYDROGEN LAYER

2000

1500

HELIUM LAYER

1000

500

OXYGEN LAYER

0        LOWER ATMOSPHERE

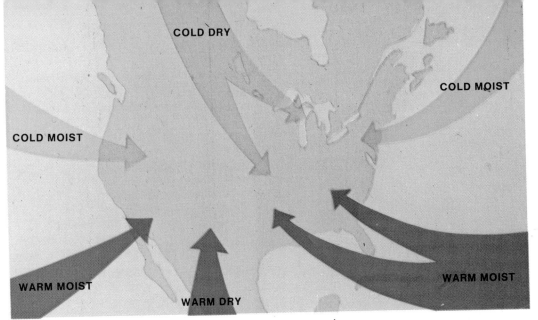

COLD DRY

COLD MOIST

COLD MOIST

WARM MOIST

WARM DRY

WARM MOIST

Currents of air affect changes in temperature and bring moisture to dry areas.

The balance among gases and forces of the earth's atmosphere is a part of the miraculous pattern of the universe. Because the balance of gases in the atmosphere differs from that in areas surrounding other planets, one wonders whether life on other planets is possible. This balance seems to maintain itself through the proper number of plants and animals on Earth.

If the air stopped moving, no wind would blow life-giving warm air into the frigid regions, or bring life-saving cool air to the unbearably hot tropical regions. There would be no medium to carry moisture from the sea to the thirsty land.

The sun is the source of ENERGY that causes winds. Radiant energy from the sun falls upon the earth. Some of the energy, while passing through the air, is turned into heat energy, but most of it passes through the air to the earth. A small amount of radiant energy is reflected by the clouds and the earth and is lost in space. Unequal heating of the earth and water causes the air to move in the form of wind from place to place. The rotation of the earth influences the wind's direction. Land heats more rapidly than water, and the air over land becomes warmer than the air over water. The cooler air is more dense and exerts greater pressure than the warmer expanded air. The cooler air flows toward the regions of warm air and forces the warm air upward. This upward movement of air is called *convection*. Violent convection currents of air, with downdrafts of cooler air cause thunderstorms.

Air is a mixture of gases and various impurities. In proportion, the gases are approximately 78% nitrogen, 21% oxygen, and 1% other gases. Air also contains variable amounts of water vapor. The table on the preceding page is a more precise analysis of the gases in air.

Much knowledge about the nature of gases was revealed through the studies of ROBERT BOYLE, around the middle of the 17th century, and by JACQUES CHARLES about one hundred years later. They explored the relationships of volume, pressure, and temperature, and laid the foundations for present day analysis of air movements.

The phenomenon of AIR PRESSURE and density was explained as early as 1643 by the Italian Torricelli, whose famous experiments with a glass tube filled with mercury made possible the measuring of variations in air pressure.

Oxygen, the gas needed to support life, was not always an ingredient of the atmosphere. In the past history of the earth, oxygen appeared long after most of the other gases that now make up the atmosphere.

## ORIGIN

The origin of the atmosphere is, of course, a part of the origin of the earth. That event is estimated to have taken place about four or five billion years ago, and under conditions which caused the earth to be extremely hot. Air, as man knows it, was not around the earth, only a thick mass of hot gases, probably highly poisonous. The great

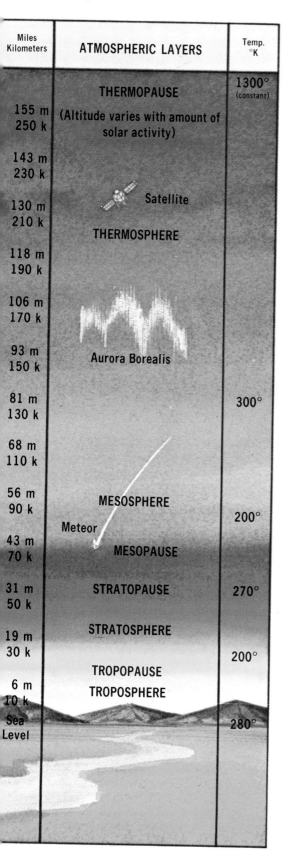

| Miles Kilometers | ATMOSPHERIC LAYERS | Temp. °K |
|---|---|---|
| | THERMOPAUSE | 1300° (constant) |
| 155 m 250 k | (Altitude varies with amount of solar activity) | |
| 143 m 230 k | | |
| 130 m 210 k | Satellite | |
| | THERMOSPHERE | |
| 118 m 190 k | | |
| 106 m 170 k | | |
| 93 m 150 k | Aurora Borealis | |
| 81 m 130 k | | 300° |
| 68 m 110 k | | |
| 56 m 90 k | MESOSPHERE | |
| 43 m 70 k | Meteor | 200° |
| | MESOPAUSE | |
| 31 m 50 k | STRATOPAUSE | 270° |
| 19 m 30 k | STRATOSPHERE | |
| | | 200° |
| 6 m 10 k | TROPOPAUSE TROPOSPHERE | |
| Sea Level | | 280° |

velocity of the gas molecules, because of high temperature, allowed most of them to escape the gravitational field into outer space.

As the earth grew colder, changes took place on its crust and in its atmosphere. Water vapor, nitrogen and carbon dioxide which had been dissolved in the liquid rock began to fill the air. In modern times, volcanic eruptions give some idea of the composition of the atmosphere at this stage of its development. It was still highly poisonous.

Eventually rain reached the earth, forming rivers, lakes and oceans. Large amounts of carbon dioxide in the atmosphere became part of the earth's crust or dissolved in the oceans. The components which were to make the development of life possible in later ages were already evident in the atmosphere, according to such scientists as Oparin and Urey. Then the thick dark clouds surrounding the earth parted and allowed sunlight to penetrate for the first time. There followed a period of gigantic storms and great upheaval. During this time, organic substances entered their first phase. Then oxygen made its appearance. How it arrived upon the scene at the right time is the subject of a number of theories, but it is certain that once oxygen was present in the atmosphere, the evolution of higher life and man from primitive cells was possible.

## LAYERS

The atmosphere may be divided into layers, or zones, each with its own characteristics. The layer which people move about in every day, and which is said to extend to an elevation of about 35,000 feet or 10,668 meters is called the *troposphere.* This is a suitable name because troposphere means "region of turning, or change," and in this layer weather changes take place. Above it is a thin layer, the *tropopause,* that separates the troposphere from the stratosphere. The name *stratosphere* comes from the Latin word *stratum,* meaning "layer." Above the stratosphere are three more layers—the stratopause, the mesophere, and the thermosphere.

The height of the troposphere varies with latitude and from season to season. At the poles its height averages 5 miles (8 kilometers) at the equator 11 miles (18 kilometers) and at the middle latitudes about 7 miles (11 kilometers). Generally, the warmer the climate at the surface of the earth, the higher the troposphere. This is caused by the heating of the air, which makes it less dense. The seasonal change in the height is caused by seasonal differences in the heating of the atmosphere.

It is within the troposphere that all of the earth's weather is formed. It is a region of clouds and ever-changing weather conditions. The name troposphere is derived from the Greek work *tropikos,* meaning "turn," because the atmosphere is always turning up in great currents. As one would move from the surface of the earth up through the troposphere, two distinct changes would be observed. Both the *temperature and pressure would decrease with increasing altitude.* In still air, the temperature decrease would be 3½° F. per 1,000 feet (1.1° C. per 304.8 meters) increase in altitude. This is called the normal lapse rate and is caused by a decrease in air density. The molecules of air are farther apart the higher you go. The standard air pressure at sea level is 29.92 inches (76 centimeters) of mercury, at 35,000 feet (10,668 meters) it is 7.0 inches (17.8 centimeters).

The stratosphere extends from the troposphere to a height of about 30 miles (48.28 kilometers) above the earth. As its name indicates, it is a region of horizontal, or layer-like, air movement. Here the winds are always strong and steady. There is no dust or water vapor, and therefore the skies are always clear. For this reason many of the commercial airlines fly in this zone. However, aircraft passengers must be protected from the extremes of temperature and low pressure.

At the bottom part of the stratosphere the temperature is very low, an average of about -67° F. (-55° C.) in the middle latitudes. Recent observations have shown that the temperature starts to rise until the 28-mile (45.06-kilometer) level is reached. Here the temperature may be 90° F. (32.2° C.) or higher. It then falls again to well below freezing at the 50-mile (80.47-kilometer) level. It marks the top of the

stratosphere. This level is known as the stratopause.

In the stratosphere exists a layer called the *ozonosphere.* In this layer the thermometer shows an increase in temperature and it puzzles meterologists. All the physiochemical reactions which take place in this area are far from being understood, but it is known that the action of short-wave RADIATION on the oxygen molecules causes them to split and form a new substance, OZONE. During the process, heat is liberated to the extent the thermometer rises to more than 30° C. at 32 miles up (86° F. at 51.5 kilometers). Although the ozone formed is itself poisonous, this layer is called a life-saving one, because the damaging ultra-violet rays from the sun lose much of their power here when they become involved in converting oxygen into ozone. Animal and plant life is again protected and preserved.

Within the mesosphere and thermosphere is a region of air that has a large number of electrically charged air molecules called ions. This is the ionosphere. These ions are the cause of unusual electrical effects. Ions appear to collect in layers, each layer having somewhat different characteristics. At some levels of the ionosphere the ions reflect certain types of radio waves. It is in the ionosphere that we see the great display of the northern lights or *aurora borealis.* In the Southern Hemisphere the lights are called *aurora australis.* The ions are electrically excited by certain types of radiation given off by the sun, the ions in turn giving off light energy. The occurrence of the aurora is linked with the cycle of sunspots on the sun.

On the outer edge of the atmosphere, the air trails thinly into space, much as the smoke of a campfire seems to float outward and disappear into the air. The gravitational pull at this point acts very weakly on the air particles, some of them escaping into outer space, others bouncing back into lower layers. This last layer is called thermosphere because of the extremely high temperatures there. A final ozone layer which marks a transition from the atmosphere to the thin gas beyond is called the *exosphere.* Beyond this, SPACE begins.

Space is defined as the area beyond the earth's atmosphere or beyond the solar system. Space has no limits.                    E.M.N.

SEE ALSO: EARTH, SPACE MEDICINE

Atolls are built up bit by bit as coral skeletons are deposited

**Atoll** (AT-ol) An atoll is an ISLAND built by tiny animals that live in warm ocean waters. These are called coral animals and their skeletons form coral rock. CORAL is formed where water is not deep. Coral islands or atolls may be formed on tops of underwater mountains or old volcanoes that are just below the surface. Coral is built up on these mountain tops for many years until it comes to the surface.

An atoll is either circular or horse-shoe in shape and surrounds a calm lagoon. The islands range from 1 to 100 miles (1.609 to 160.9 kilometers) around. The depth of the lagoons are from about 100 to 300 feet (30.5 to 91.4 meters). Atolls are found by the thousands in the tropical areas of the Indian and Pacific oceans.

CHARLES DARWIN'S explanation of their formation is the most believable. First of all, coral animals build a reef along the shore line of a volcanic peak. Then wind and rain gradually wear down and eventually destroy this peak. The reef continues to grow upward, however, only a few feet above the surrounding water. At last only the coral reef remains surrounding the sunken island.

Only a few things live on an atoll. COCONUT palms, breadfruit trees, and PANDANUS trees comprise the plant life. Rats and land crabs are the only animals. Fish can be found in great quantity in the lagoon and the surrounding waters of the reef.

Since the 1940's atolls have achieved some prominence, for it was on Eniwetok and Bikini atolls, for instance, that the atomic and hydrogen bomb experiments took place.                    D. E. Z.

**Atom** Matter is composed of *molecules*. Molecules are composed of *atoms*. Atoms are composed of *protons, neutrons,* and *electrons*. Many other subatomic *particles* originate in and are created by *nuclear* and atomic actions. Everything that we see about us is composed of atoms.

Generally, an atom is considered to be the smallest unit or particle of an ELEMENT which can exist and still keep the chemical and physical properties belonging to that element. Examples include IRON (solid), MERCURY (liquid), and HELIUM (gas).

Man has often wondered what would happen if he took a piece of matter and cut it into the smallest piece possible. Democritus, an ancient Greek, reasoned that if you did continue to divide matter you would eventually reach a particle that could not be divided further. He called this particle *atomos* which means indivisible.

Atoms are very small particles and only the very largest can be seen using an electron microscope. The size of atoms is expressed in terms of their radii. The radii of atoms range from .037 nanometers to .235 nanometers. ($10^9$ nanometers $= 1$ meter) The mass of atoms ranges from $1.7 \times 10^{-24}$ for hydrogen to $4.3 \times 10^{-22}$ for Hahnium.

The size of atoms makes it impossible to determine their structure directly. The structure of atoms is based on theoretical models. One of the earliest models developed by Sir J.J. Thomson (1856-1940) pictured matter as a mixture of *protons* and *electrons* like rocks and sand on a beach.

J.J. Thomson, in 1897, while working with a Crookes tube, discovered a particle that had a negative charge, the electron. In 1886, a Crookes tube with holes in its CATHODE was developed by Eugene Goldstein. It was discovered that positive particles appeared behind the cathode. When hydrogen was used in the tube, these particles were labeled as protons by Rutherford in 1914. James Chadwich (1891-1974), in

1932, while working with a highly penetrating radiation, discovered it had a mass similar to the proton but without charge, the *neutron.*

ERNEST RUTHERFORD (1871-1937) conducted a classical experiment in 1911 to test Thomson's model. In this experiment he bombarded a thin sheet of gold with *alpha particles* (sub-atomic particles). He then recorded the location of the alpha particles after he found them. Rutherford found that most of the particles passed through the foil, indicating matter is mostly empty space. A few particles bounded back towards the source, proving the mass of matter to be located in very small areas, the *nuclei.*

The number of protons in the nucleus is called the *atomic number.* This is also the number of electrons in an atom. The *mass number* for an element is given by the *atomic weight* rounded to the nearest whole number. If the atomic number is subtracted from the mass number you obtain the number of neutrons.

If electrons are either added to or subtracted from an atom, the atom becomes an *ion.* If a proton is added to an atom of an element, the type of element is changed. If a proton is added to a carbon atom with six protons, an atom of nitrogen with seven protons is formed. If neutrons are added to an atom of an element, a new *isotope* of that element is made.

A certain amount of the mass of protons and neutrons is converted into the energy needed to hold them together. The mass-to-energy transfer is expressed by Einstein's equation. The energy used for binding is called binding energy. For an element to be stable, the ratio of neutrons to protons must be fairly constant. If this ratio is too-high or too-low the atoms of an element begin to break up. This is called *radioactivity.* A too high or too low neutron-to-proton ratio can occur naturally or artificially by adding particles to the nucleus. If an atom has many neutrons added to it, it will decay.

Some elements, such as uranium, are naturally radioactive. They throw out particles until they have enough binding energy to remain stable. Every atom of U-238 is going to throw 2 protons and 4 neutrons out of its nucleus. Each U-238 atom is going to do this just once in its entire life. But not all of the U-238 atoms are going to do this at the same time. In fact, for any one group of

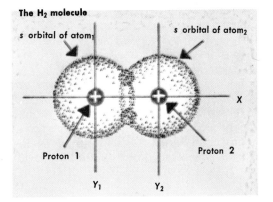

The H₂ molecule

s orbital of atom₁    s orbital of atom₂

Proton 1    Proton 2

X

Y₁    Y₂

U-238 atoms, it takes an average of 4,500,-000,000 years for one half of the uranium atoms to throw out the particles. This length of time is called the HALF-LIFE of uranium. Each radioactive element has its own half-life ranging from billions of years to billionths of seconds.

The proton-neutron ratio limits the number of elements possible. To date, man has managed to put together 105 protons to make Hahnium. No element beyond Bismuth, atomic number 83, is stable. They are all radioactive. Man might possibly make elements with more protons but they would have very short half lives, making it impossible for them to exist in nature.

In order to account for chemical activity and the characteristics spectrum of each atom, NIELS BOHR proposed that the electrons revolved around the nucleus in different orbits. Wolfgang Pauli found that within an atom no two electrons have the same amount of energy. As better spectroscopes were developed Bohr revised his model again. He stated that each electron orbit is made of sub-shells which are made of *orbitals.* Each orbital could contain any two electrons—one spinning clockwise on its axis, the other counterclockwise. The first orbit was made of one sub-shell which was made of one circular orbital. The first orbit could only contain two electrons. The second orbit was made of two sub-shells. The first sub-shell contained one circular orbital. The second sub-shell contained three elliptical orbitals. The orbit could hold only eight electrons—two in the first sub-shell and six in the second. The third orbit holds 18 electrons and fourth 32 electrons, all arranged in sub-shells and circular and varying elliptical orbitals. Recent discoveries indicate protons and neutrons in the nucleus travel in orbits, sub-shells, and orbitals.

Before the development of instruments capable of weighing an atom directly, a system of relative weights was adopted. One kind of atom was chosen as a standard and assigned an arbitrary atomic weight. All other atoms were then compared to the standard. A known volume of oxygen, the first standard, was assigned an atomic weight of 16.0000. An equal volume of hydrogen weighed 1/16 as much as the oxygen and so hydrogen's atomic weight was 1/16 of 16.0000 or 1.0000. All the other atomic weights were determined in a similar manner.

As better instruments were developed it was discovered that all atoms of the same element do not weigh the same. For example, different samples of oxygen may have an atomic weight of 16, 17, or 18. These newly discovered ISOTOPES affected the atomic weight standard. The lightest isotope of carbon was then chosen and assigned an atomic weight of 12.0000. All other atomic weights were then recomputed. Using the new standard the three isotopes of oxygen have atomic weights of 15.9962, 17.0007, and 18.0011. These three atomic weights do not appear on modern period charts. If you look for oxygen's atomic weight, you will find just one number given, 15.9994. This number is an average of all three isotopes of oxygen taking into account the relative abundance of each isotope. The lightest type of oxygen makes up 99.759 percent of the world's supply. Oxygen 17 accounts for .037 percent and oxygen 18 accounts for .204 percent.                    A.J.H./B.A.T.

SEE ALSO: ANTIMATTER, CHEMISTRY, LIGHT, MATTER, RADIOACTIVITY

## Atom smasher  see Accelerators

## Atomic bomb  see Bomb

## Atomic energy  see Nuclear energy

## Atomic number  see Atom, Elements

## Atrophy  (AT-truh-fee) Atrophy is the wasting away or decrease in size of a cell, tissue, or organ. It sometimes makes a person unable to move about or to use a part of his body.

Atrophy may be temporary, occurring after a part of the body has been disabled for some time. For example, after a leg has been broken and left in a cast for several weeks, the muscles of the leg become smaller.

The leg has to be exercised and the muscles rebuilt through use.

Atrophy of tissues also occurs when nerves supplying them are injured, severed, or affected by disease. If nerve damage is permanent, as in some cases of POLIOMYELITIS, the atrophy is progressive and cannot be stopped. When HORMONES are not circulated in large enough amounts, glands and other tissues which they govern undergo atrophy.

Also, in old age tissues tend to atrophy. The parts most affected by the atrophy of old age are the skin, reproductive organs, muscle and cartilage tissue, and occasionally the brain.                    V. V. N.

SEE ALSO: ENDOCRINE SYSTEM, MUSCLE SYSTEM

## Atropine  (AT-truh-pin) Atropine is a drug used in medicine. It is obtained from the leaves and roots of the *belladonna* plant, also known as deadly NIGHTSHADE. It has been used by physicians for many centuries.

Atropine is used to dilate the pupils of the eyes when people are examined for eyeglasses. It reduces the secretions of the glands of the body that are under the control of the AUTONOMIC NERVOUS SYSTEM. It also constricts the blood vessels, relaxes the bronchioles of the lungs, and quickens the heart beat. Atropine is helpful in treating mumps and in preparing patients for SURGERY.

Atropine has the chemical structure of an *alkaloid,* and is related to caffeine and cocaine. It is antagonistic to the effects of the parasympathetic nervous system. It blocks the action of *acetylcholine,* a *neurohormone,* which is released at the nerve ending of parasympathetic fibers in the organ cells in which the action takes place.

The pupils of the eyes become dilated because the muscles that contract the pupil are paralyzed by the atropine. The constrictor muscles of the bronchial tubes and the intestine are inhibited in the same way, so that the bronchioles and intestine are relaxed. The secretions of the salivary and other glands are also suppressed when these tissues no longer receive stimulation from the parasympathetic neurohormone.                    B. B. G.

## Attar  see Perfume

**Audubon, John James** (1785–1851)
John Audubon was an American artist who studied birds and painted them
in their natural surroundings. He explored the countryside looking for new
birds to paint. Audubon also was the
first American to put bands on the legs
of birds to find out where they flew
and how long they lived.

Audubon thought he was born in New
Orleans, Louisiana, when Louisiana was
still French territory. However, Dr. Francis
H. Herrick proved with documentary evidence that he was born in Haiti, the son of
a Creole mother and a French father who
was a mercantile agent. She seems to have
been killed in an uprising in Santa Domingo,
but the father and son escaped to France.

When he was eighteen years old, Audubon came to America to live on his father's
estate near Philadelphia. There he began
to paint birds from life. That same year he
carried on the first bird-banding experiment
in the United States.

In 1808 Audubon married and ten years
later moved to Kentucky. This move proved
important in his life because in Louisville,
Kentucky, he met Alexander Wilson, the
first American *ornithologist,* or student of
birds. He showed Audubon the first two
volumes of his study of birds entitled
*American Ornithology.*

Audubon's primary interest in life was
painting birds in their natural surroundings,
He rebelled against painting stuffed birds
mounted for museum use, as was the cus-
tom of his day. He loved to explore the
fields, the hills and the woodlands, looking
for new birds to observe and to paint.

In 1826 Audubon went to England to
exhibit his drawings of birds and to find a
publisher. He later published the drawings
in a huge volume entitled *The Birds of
America.* This work contained 435 life-
sized colored pictures of birds. In 1839,
with the help of William MacGillivray,
Audubon published *Ornithological Biogra-
phy,* a descriptive explanation of American
birds. His reputation was later established
when he published *Synopsis of the Birds of
North America.* Audubon then settled on
his estate, now Aubudon Park, New York,
to enjoy his last years observing and drawing birds.          D. H. J.

The razor-billed auk (top) shares its habitat with
its relative the puffin (bottom). The flightless
great auk is now extinct

**Auk** (AWK) Auks are large diving
birds in the same group (order) with
gulls, snipes, sandpipers, and plovers.
Their bodies are heavy. Their necks
are short with large heads. Beaks are
parrot-like and toes are webbed. The
hind toe is absent or reduced in size.
Bodies are dark on top and white
underneath. Though they are powerful divers, they appear awkward in
the air or on land. They usually dive
for food, eating crustaceans (crab,
shrimp, crayfish) and plankton. The
word plankton refers to all small floating plants and animals on the surface
of the sea.

The 22 species of auks range along the
coasts of the northern Pacific, Atlantic, and
Arctic oceans. They all breed in large colonies on cliffs, wintering on the open sea.

The Great Auk has been extinct since
1844. It was flightless and easily captured. It
was killed for its oil and feathers.     J. C. K.

**Aureomycin**  see Antibiotics

**Auricle**  see Heart

**The Charioteer**

**Auriga** (aw-RY-gah) Auriga is a group of stars that is thought to resemble the driver of a chariot. The main stars of this CONSTELLATION form a five-sided figure in the sky. There is one very bright star in this group. Its name is *Capella*. Near Capella are three fainter stars that form a small triangle. These are called *The Kids*. The best time to look for The Charioteer is in winter.

Traditionally, the Charioteer is supposed to represent the first chariot-driver, Erichthonius. Erichthonius was the son of Vulcan and Minerva. Because he was crippled and could not get around very well, he invented the horse-drawn chariot. In recognition of this invention, a memorial to him was made in the heavens. Some legends say that the charioteer is Phaeton, the son of Apollo. One day Phaeton borrowed Apollo's chariot, and when he tried to drive it, he was overturned. Capella, the bright, beautiful yellow star, is sometimes called The Goat. The goat and her kids were given a place in the stars because the king of the gods, Jupiter, was supposed to have drunk goat's milk as a baby. Ancient Hebrews called this constellation The Good Shepherd.     C. L. K.

**Aurora borealis** (uh-RORE-ruh boh-ree-AL-iss) An aurora borealis is a beautiful display of moving colored lights in the northern night sky. It is sometimes called the Northern Lights. Auroras in the southern part of the world are called the Southern Lights or *aurora australis*. The two are both called *aurora polaris*.

Auroras occur about 60 miles (96.56 kilometers) above the earth and may extend for hundreds of miles upward. They are most often green or yellow-green, yellow, and red. Sometimes shades of blue, gray and violet also are seen. The shapes and movements vary widely.

Auroras are believed to be related to sunspots, storms on the sun that send off electrical particles. Auroras occur where the atmosphere is very thin. There is almost a VACUUM there. When these particles reach the thin atmosphere, they cause the rarefied gases to glow. The varied colors are probably created by the interaction of the electrified particles from the sun with different kinds of gases.

The theory that auroras are electric displays is supported by the fact that they bear a consistent relationship to the magnetic poles. There are definite areas near the north and south poles where auroras occur most frequently. The best area to observe auroras in the northern hemisphere is around the Hudson Bay, where auroras occur about two out of every three nights. Auroras can be seen fairly often in the northern United States. On rare occasions they have been seen even as far south as Florida or Louisiana.     C. L. K.

**Aurora borealis, or Northern Lights, is a display of color seen in the sky**

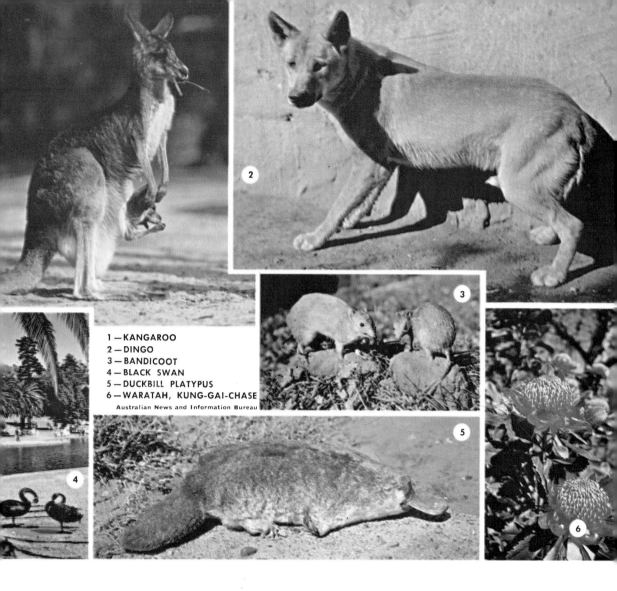

1 — KANGAROO
2 — DINGO
3 — BANDICOOT
4 — BLACK SWAN
5 — DUCKBILL PLATYPUS
6 — WARATAH, KUNG-GAI-CHASE
Australian News and Information Bureau

**Australia** Australia is the smallest CONTINENT, but it is the world's largest island. Its area is about 3,000,000 square miles (7,769,970 square kilometers), or ⅙ less than the United States. It lies south of the equator and south of ASIA. It is completely surrounded by the waters of the southwest Pacific Ocean and the southeast Indian Ocean. Australia is very far from other lands except Southeast Asia and the south Pacific islands. By air, Melbourne is almost 8,000 miles (12,875 kilometers) from California, over 7,000 miles (11,265 kilometers) from Brazil, 6,000 miles (9,656 kilometers) from Bombay, India, and 5,000 miles (8,047 kilometers) from Tokyo, Japan.

Australia is a land of strange animals and plants such as the KANGAROO and EUCALYPTUS. They are found nowhere else. Its native people, or *aborigines,* had a very primitive culture before the coming of the settlers. This was because of the great distance between them and other peoples from whom they might have learned new ideas. The aborigines live on reservations in the northern tropical region.

### LAND FORMS

The central and western parts of Australia are a great PLATEAU with an average eleva-

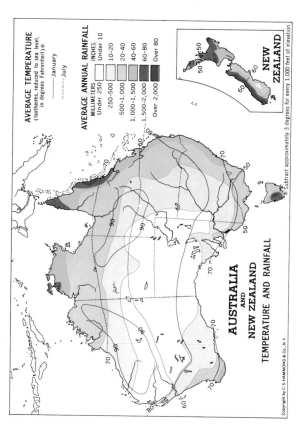

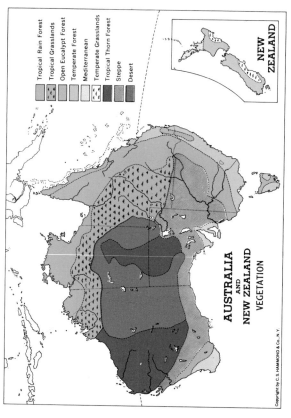

tion of 1,000 feet (305 meters.) Toward the west and northwest, upland ranges may reach 4,000 feet (1,219 meters.) Eastward from the plateau is a great basin. This plains region is far from being entirely flat. Toward the eastern coast, a great dividing range of mountains runs north and south. The highest peak in this range is Mt. Kosciusko, over 7,300 feet (2225 meters). The Great Dividing Range has various local names such as the Australian Alps and the Liverpool Range. The width of the mountains is about 150 miles (241 kilometers).

A coastal plain lies adjacent to the Pacific Ocean. Its width varies from 50-300 miles (80.5-482.8 kilometers). Along the coast is the *Great Barrier Reef,* the longest reef in the world—more than 1250 miles (2012 kilometers) long. The outer face just below the surface is composed of actively growing CORAL. A protected channel for ships lies between this and the shore. At times, tides and hidden rocks make the channel dangerous.

The 12,000 mile (19,312 kilometer) coast line of Australia is relatively smooth. There are only two large arms of the sea. In the north, the Gulf of Carpentaria lies between Yorke Peninsula and Arnhem Land. In the south, an inlet known as the Great Australian Bight lies along the middle of the coastline. However, there are several good harbors. Sydney, on the southeast coast, has a great harbor.

## CLIMATE

Australia has many CLIMATES. A rainy tropical climate is found in a small section of the northeast coast. Here the rainfall is heavy, with temperatures only moderately high. Over a greater coastal area in the north, the climate is monsoon tropical with a wet and dry season similar to the climate of most of India. The rainy season comes in November until the end of April. This is summer in Australia.

In a wide belt from the west coast to the mountains along the east is a semi-arid tropical climate. Rainfall varies from 10-20 inches (25.4-51 centimeters) annually, and the rainy season is much shorter than in the monsoon region to the north. Temperatures are high throughout the year, the averages ranging from 75°-95° F. (23.9°-35° C.).

The great Victoria Desert occupies central and western Australia. The climate

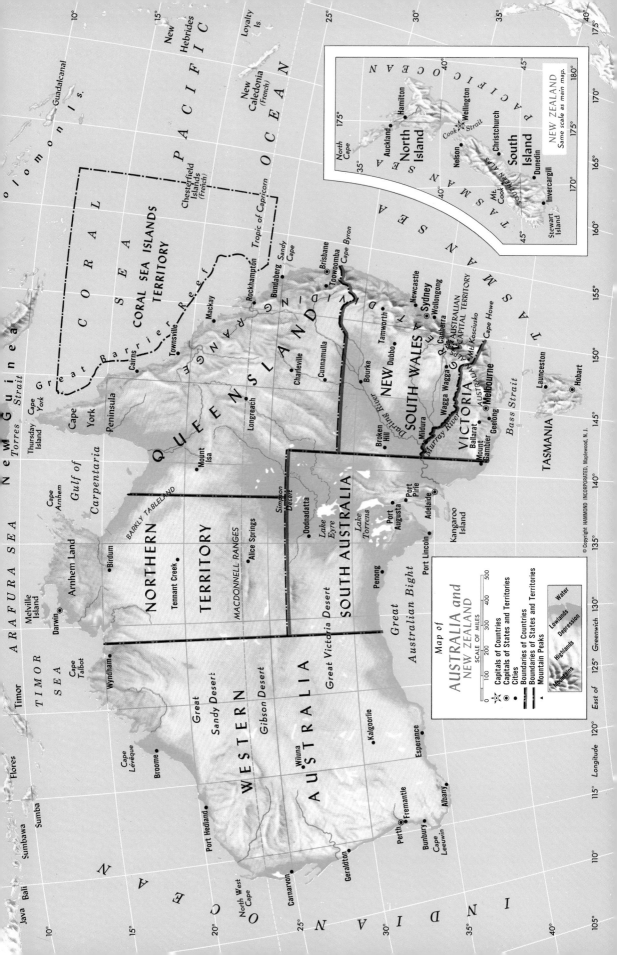

PACIFIC OCEAN

New Hebrides

Loyalty Is.

New Caledonia (French)

Solomon Is.

Guadalcanal

New Guinea

TIMOR SEA

ARAFURA SEA

Java
Bali
Sumba
Sumbawa
Flores

Timor

Cape Talbot

Cape Leveque

Broome

Port Hedland

North West Cape

Carnarvon

Geraldton

Cape Leeuwin

Bunbury

Perth
Fremantle

Albany

Esperance

Kalgoorlie

Wiluna

WESTERN AUSTRALIA

Great Sandy Desert

Gibson Desert

Great Victoria Desert

Penong

Great Australian Bight

Port Lincoln

Kangaroo Island

Adelaide

Port Augusta

Port Pirie

Lake Torrens

Lake Eyre

Oodnadatta

SOUTH AUSTRALIA

Simpson Desert

NORTHERN TERRITORY

MACDONNELL RANGES

Alice Springs

Tennant Creek

Birdum

Darwin

Melville Island

Cape Arnhem

Arnhem Land

Wyndham

BARKLY TABLELAND

Gulf of Carpentaria

Cape York

Peninsula

Thursday Island

Cape York

Torres Strait

Mount Isa

Longreach

QUEENSLAND

Charleville

Cunnamulla

Bourke

Broken Hill

Mildura

Wagga Wagga

Murray River

Darling River

VICTORIA

Ballarat

Geelong

Melbourne

Mount Gambier

Bass Strait

TASMANIA

Launceston

Hobart

NEW SOUTH WALES

Dubbo

Tamworth

Newcastle

Sydney

Wollongong

Canberra
AUSTRALIAN CAPITAL TERRITORY

Mt. Kosciusko

Cape Howe

GREAT DIVIDING RANGE

Brisbane
Toowoomba

Cape Byron

Bundaberg

Sandy Cape

Rockhampton

Mackay

Townsville

Cairns

Great Barrier Reef

CORAL SEA

CORAL SEA ISLANDS TERRITORY

Chesterfield Islands (French)

Tropic of Capricorn

TASMAN SEA

© Copyright HAMMOND INCORPORATED, Maplewood, N.J.

INDIAN OCEAN

East of Greenwich
Longitude

NEW ZEALAND

North Cape

Auckland

Hamilton

Wellington

Cook Strait

Nelson

Christchurch

Dunedin

Invercargill

Stewart Island

SOUTHERN ALPS

Mt. Cook

North Island

South Island

PACIFIC OCEAN

TASMAN SEA

NEW ZEALAND
Same scale as main map.

Cockatiel

Wombat

Common heath

here is arid tropical. The driest parts receive less than 5 inches (12 centimeters) of rain a year. Parts of the desert region are named the Great Sandy Desert, the Gibson, and the Simpson. This great desert is part of uninhabited Australia and, together with some marginal lands, where only 25,000 settlers live, constitutes at least half of Australia.

Along the southern coast toward the west and the east, a Mediterranean subtropical climate is found. Most of the rainfall is in the winter. Winters are mild although the temperature may occasionally fall below freezing. Summers are hot. Most of the east coast area of Australia has a humid subtropical climate similar to that of Florida. Rainfall is adequate and falls in every month. Most Australians live along the east coast.

Along the coast of southeast Australia is the temperate marine climate similar to that of Washington and Oregon. Melbourne, in southern Victoria, Tasmania, and New Zealand all have a temperate marine climate. Rainfall is abundant.

### RIVERS AND DRAINAGE

The Murray-Darling river system is the largest drainage system in Australia. Its length is about 2,300 miles (3701.5 kilometers). The Murray-Darling drains the great central basin. Its waters provide irrigation and generation of electric power. Many rivers in the arid interior merely disappear in the dry soil over which they flow. Rivers along the north coast in the monsoon rainy season may be big, but in the dry season they are almost dry. The short rivers which drain the eastern slopes of the Great Dividing Range run into the Coral Sea. Those which drain the southeastern slopes run into the Tasman Sea.

### PLANTS AND ANIMALS

Because Australia is so isolated from the other continents, it has many unique animals and plant forms. The platypus, or DUCKBILL, is a small egg-laying aquatic mammal with a bill like a duck's, webbed feet, a tail like a beaver's and fur like a mole's. It provides its young with milk. It is probably a link between mammals and earlier forms in the history of EVOLUTION.

A famous tree native to Australia is the eucalyptus. It can live and flourish in arid (dry) lands when other plants fail to survive. It sends roots down and out many times longer than its trunk. The eucalyptus has been planted for shade in arid regions of the American southwest and elsewhere with success.

Australia is best known for the kangaroo, a member of the MARSUPIAL family. Actually, there are many types and sizes of kangaroo. The large kangaroos and wallaroos are often found in zoos around the world. The hind feet of adults measure over 10 inches (25.4 centimeters). The large hind legs and the long powerful tail account for the kangaroo's ten-

The koala, the "teddy bear" of Australia

dency toward an erect stance and for its ability to leap long distances. It has relatively small front feet. The WALLABY is a smaller kangaroo with hind feet which measure from 6-10 inches (15.2-25.4 centimeters.) A tree-climbing kangaroo is smaller still with front and hind feet almost equal in size and a less powerful tail. Kangaroos eat plants. Females carry their young in a pouch.

The KOALA BEAR, a tree-climbing marsupial, is native to the wet temperate areas of the southeast. The koala is a double for the toy "teddy bear" given to children in Europe and America. It grows to a height of slightly over 2 feet (.61 meters.) The cub spends the first six months of its life in its mother's pouch. The koala eats the leaves and tender shoots of some species of the eucalyptus tree.

Native to Australia also are two strange flightless birds, the lyre and the emu. The former mimics the sounds made by other birds and animals. It spreads its tail feathers in the shape of a lyre. The emu is a large bird related to the ostrich and grows to a height of over 6 feet (1.8 meters.)

Australia has both deciduous and coniferous forests of commercial value on the mountains and plains near the east, southeast, and southwest coasts. The flora of the northern coastal areas is tropical. That of the arid interior is typical of desert areas.

### NATURAL RESOURCES

Certain areas of Australia receive their water supply from artesian bores. The Great Artesian Basin (about 676,250 square miles or 1,751,481 square kilometers) is the most extensive in the world. Large industrial cities draw their water from rivers and from man-made rainfall storages.

Lumber from the mountains and coastal plains is of significant value.

Gold is an important resource. Other minerals of importance are coal, oil, zinc, silver, uranium, lead, copper, and iron. Most of Australia's wealth comes from sheep, cattle, and farm products. One-fourth of the world's wool comes from this continent, and wheat is an important crop.

Australia has become a world leader in the production of raw materials.        J.H.D.

SEE ALSO: DESERT, EARTH, GEOGRAPHY, NATURAL RESOURCES

**Autogiro** (otto-JY-row) An autogiro (sometimes called a *gyroplane*) is an AIRCRAFT which belongs to the rotating wing family. The craft has a body, or fuselage, somewhat like an ordinary small AIRPLANE, but it also has a large propeller (called a *rotor*) mounted horizontally, like an umbrella, overhead.

Except for the appearance of the overhead rotor, the autogiro bears little resemblance to the HELICOPTER. The rotor on the autogiro is tilted back slightly and is not usually connected to the engine which turns the front propeller. As the plane begins to move forward for the take-off, the force of the air coming under the front part of the rotor blades provides a lifting force as it does to a stationary wing. The forward motion starts the rotor to rotate. Sometimes the rotor is power-driven only at take-off to give faster vertical lift. The rotor blades are hinged at the rotor hub so that as the air forces change. This natural action gives the autogiro the ability to take off and land with little or no ground roll. It can also fly as slowly as 20 mph (32.2 kph).        E.I.D

SEE ALSO: GYROSCOPE

**Automatic pilot** see Instrument panel

**Automatic sprinkler** see Fire extinguishers

Inland Steel

**Automatic control lets men work with ore dust that once was discarded as hazardous**

**Automation** Automation is a way of manufacturing things or doing work with little or no human help. Once applied almost exclusively to manufacturing assembly lines, automation is today sweeping throughout society. Many consumer products—from television sets and automobiles to microwave ovens and home computers—are automating household and recreational tasks formerly performed only by humans.

### HISTORY

As early as 1784, Oliver Evans built an automatic flour mill outside Philadelphia. In 1801, Joseph Marie Jacquard built a loom which was run from a system of punched cards that became so popular that over a thousand of these machines were sold in France alone. The punched card system of automatic control was not revived again until after World War II, when it was recognized as a means of supplying information to large electronic COMPUTERS.

Probably one of the earliest automatic control devices was the governor on the steam engine built by JAMES WATT. This device used centrifugal force to regulate the amount of steam supplied to the driving piston. Other examples of early attempts at automation are ELI WHITNEY's cotton gin; the reaper, invented by Cyrus McCormick; and the repeating rifle, manufactured and made famous by Winchester Repeating Arms Company in Massachusetts. These inventions represent attempts at automation in three different areas. The cotton gin was

**Plastic cans wait to be filled in a petroleum products factory.**

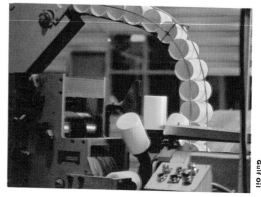

Gulf Oil

one of the first semiautomatic processes in industry. The reaper was the beginning of highly mechanized farming, and the repeating rifle completely changed the tactics employed in warfare.

Henry Ford probably had the most to do with the automation of an entire manufacturing process. He revolutionized the automobile industry by his introduction of assembly line methods. Today, very few products are not built or processed by assembly line techniques.

### AUTOMATIC CONTROL

Control can be as simple as flicking the switch that turns an electric light on or off or it can be as complex as the inertial guidance systems that keep the large satellite rockets on course.

In the driveway of a home, a light on a pole operated by a time clock in the basement is analogous to what is called *open-loop control.* Here, on and off is the only process one may wish to exercise with a control. One of the most important advantages of the open-loop system is that the control itself may be placed at a great distance from the object or machine it controls.

There are, however, many disadvantages to the open-loop system. These make the exclusive use of this system difficult in most applications of automation. For instance, in this example it would be most desirable to have the control clock turn the driveway light on when the sun sets and turn it off when the sun rises the next morning. But this is not possible in an open-loop control system. Since the open-loop system has no methods of correcting errors that have been made in control, a system that could correct errors had to be devised. There is, in automation, a system called *closed-loop* control, which extends far beyond the limitations of the open-loop controls. An example of the closed-loop control is a thermostat, used to regulate temperatures. Here, the only human operation setting performed is the dial at a desired temperature. When the temperature in the room drops below the

Courtesy Pfizer Inc.

desired level, the thermostat "tells" the furnace that heat is needed in that area. After the furnace has delivered a sufficient amount of heat, the thermostat again "tells" the furnace that the room is at the desired temperature, and the furnace shuts itself off. This differs from the time clock and light-control system because the thermostat called for heat only when needed, regardless of whether that might be day or night.

A very efficient control system is developed by the combination of the open- and closed-loop systems. Steering an automobile can be considered a combination of the two systems. The steering wheel turns the car left or right, an open-loop system. The closed system component is provided when the driver adjusts the direction of the car to meet the situation. For example, he can steer around a dog in the street and return to his own lane.

Since the early 1980s, office automation has been revolutionizing the way businesses communicate inside their own offices and with other firms. Secretaries now type correspondence on word processors, a specialized type of computer. What is typed into the computer appears on the screen of a video-display terminal (VDT). An executive can push a button and view on a VDT screen located in his or her office what the secretary has typed. All or part of the message can be changed merely by typing appropriate commands onto a keyboard terminal. The computer interprets the typed commands, corrects the original message, and then appropriately alters what is displayed on the screens. Finished correspondance can be sent in seconds to VDTs in other offices throughout the world. Alternatively, these messages can be printed without error by computer-controlled office printers, at double, or better, the speed of the best human typists.

**Autobac I tests bacterial susceptibility to antibiotics automatically.**

Automation allows business executives to meet with people in other cities without leaving their own offices. Through this kind of teleconferencing, images and the speech of participants are relayed to other offices. Executives in one city can even write on special chalkboards and have their messages seen immediately in other cities.

Both offices and industry are using computer-operated robots. Some offices, for example, use robots to deliver mail. In industry, "smart" (computer-operated) production monitors respond to voice commands of human inspectors to change the operation of assembly-line robots.

Even the art of animation has become automated. There are usually 12 individual cartoon drawings (frames) needed for each second of film. With the computer's help, artists now sketch a cartoon's outlines for the key frames only. The computer fills in the outlines with colors selected by the artist and then with minimal direction draws the additional frames needed. For example, to make a cartoon character sit up in bed, the artist outlines the character lying down in one key frame, then sketches the character sitting up in another frame. The computer draws the frames that show the character rising into the sitting position. Today automation allows animated cartoons that would have taken months to draw in the 1950s to be produced in a few hours.

H.P.O./A.J.H

The panel at the left provides control, through automation, of all the operations in an entire steel production plant (right). Men work in safer conditions when dangerous operations are handled automatically

Inland Steel

Ford Taurus

Honda Accord SE Sedan

**Automobile** The automobile is the most important land vehicle ever built on earth. In many nations, it is the primary means of land travel today. The automobile is constantly being improved to make it safer, more comfortable, more energy efficient, and less polluting.

The very first automobile was invented more than two hundred years ago in France. It was a primitive vehicle with steam power and wooden wheels. Revolutionary changes have resulted in today's automobile with its gasoline engine, transmission, brakes, steel belted rubber tires, and body made with steel, glass, plastic, and aluminum.

### THE ENGINE

The ENGINE is the heart of the automobile. It provides the power that turns the wheels. Its major parts are the pistons and cylinders, the connecting rods, the crankshaft, the fuel system, the ignition system, the cooling system, and the lubrication system. This type of engine is called an *internal-combustion* engine.

Nearly all gasoline automobile engines operate on four strokes and are called *four-cycle* engines. The first stroke of the *piston* in the

*cylinder* draws in the fuel mixture of gasoline and air. The second stroke compresses the fuel mixture. A carefully timed spark from a *spark plug* ignites the fuel and forces a third stroke. The fourth stroke removes the waste gases in the cylinder through the *exhaust valve*, the exhaust pipe, the *muffler* and *catalytic converter*, and the *tail pipe*.

General Motors Corporation

This 1992 Oldsmobile engine has 16 valves and fuel injection.

Winton

1886 Benz

1903 Model A Ford

Automobile Quarterly

Duesenberg J Coupe

Auburn-Cord-Duesenberg Museum/© Nicky Wright

1947 Volkswagen Beetle

National Motor Museum/© Nicky Wright

Far left: 1957 Thunderbird

Left: 1953 Chevrolet Corvette

Below: 1957 Chevrolet Bel-Air convertible

...ord-Duesenberg Museum/Nicky Wright

National Motor Museum/© Nicky Wright

Right: Mercedes-Benz 600SL

Below: 1993 Lexus LS 400

Courtesy Chrysler Corporation

...otor Sales USA, Inc./Lexus Division

Mercedes-Benz of North America, Inc.

1992 Dodge Viper

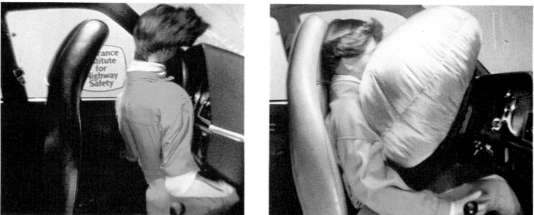

Without an airbag (left) the driver runs the risk of fatal injury. The presence of an airbag (right) significantly increases the driver's chance of survival.

Each piston in the engine works up and down in its individual cylinder. When the piston is pushed downward by the force of the explosion of fuel in the cylinder on its third stroke, it pushes the *connecting rod* which, in turn, rotates the *crankshaft*. The revolving crankshaft is connected to the mechanisms that turn the automobile's wheels. Modern automobiles have four, six, or eight cylinders.

The *fuel system* in most modern automobiles uses gasoline. The gasoline is stored in the fuel tank. A *fuel pump* pushes the gasoline through pipes into *fuel injectors* which vaporize the gasoline and mix it with air. This explosive mixture is drawn into each cylinder during its intake stroke. In order to reduce the emission of air pollutants from the fuel system, a *positive crankcase ventilator (PCV)* was added to American-built automobiles.

*Ignition systems* in American-built cars have an a.c. (alternating current) generator called an *alternator*; a *battery*; a *distributor*; and *spark plugs*, among other components. All are part of a complex electrical system that provides the energy to start the engine, to continue igniting the fuel, and to operate accessories such as the radio and headlights. The alternator uses the mechanical motion of the engine to generate electricity, some of which is stored in the battery as chemical energy. This energy provides electrical current to the ignition system. The battery and alternator provide the electrical current which travels through the wires to the spark coil. This coil provides the high voltage needed for the spark.

The *cooling system* of most automobiles uses water mixed with additives to prevent rust and freezing. Since the constant explosion of fuel at more than 3500° F (1927° C) would soon damage the engine, circulating water is used to keep the cylinder temperatures around 200° F (93° C). The water is moved by a circulating pump through hollow channels *(water jackets)* surrounding the cylinders. From there, the heated water circulates to the *radiator* by connecting hoses. In its passage through the honeycomb cells of the radiator, the water is cooled by outside air pulled in by a fan operating directly behind the radiator. The cool water then recirculates through the engine's water jackets. A *thermostat* causes the water passage between the radiator and the engine to open and close to keep the water and engine parts at the best operating temperatures.

The *lubrication system* reduces friction by distributing oil from the reservoir in the *crankcase* to all engine parts where friction may occur. The movement of the crankshaft in the crankcase splashes oil to such areas as the crankshaft bearings, connecting rod bearings, the pistons, and cylinder walls. An *oil pump* forces more oil through channels and pipes to other parts of the engine where friction occurs.

Most modern cars have a number of anti-pollution devices. The positive crankcase ventilator (PCV) reduces the emission of hydrocarbons from the fuel system. The *catalytic converter* reduces exhaust emissions of carbon monoxide and nitrogen oxides. Cars with catalytic converters must burn unleaded gasoline.

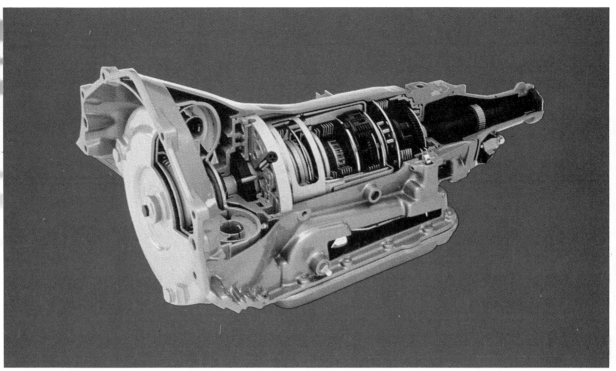

**Oldsmobile electronic transmission**

General Motors Corporation

## TRANSMISSION

The engine power is transmitted to the wheels through the *clutch*, the *transmission*, the *drive shaft*, and the *differential*. Most modern automobiles utilize the front wheels as drive wheels. Some models apply drive power to the rear wheels or, in the case of four-wheel-drive vehicles, to both the front and rear wheels.

Clutches provide the connecting power link between the engine crankshaft and the *drive train*. They may be mechanical *friction clutches* or *hydraulic clutches*. They both have metal disks that move apart or come together when the gears are shifted from one driving range to another, such as from neutral to low gear, or from neutral to reverse.

A transmission is usually directly behind the clutch. A *manual transmission* contains gears of different sizes. With this type of transmission, the driver uses a *gearshift lever* to select the proper forward or reverse gears. The car begins moving forward in low gear. As the speed increases, the driver must release the clutch by pushing down on the clutch pedal, move the transmission into second gear by moving the transmission lever, and finally re-engage the clutch by allowing the clutch pedal to move upward. The process is repeated for a third, and sometimes four or more forward gears as the automobile accelerates.

Most modern automobiles now use *automatic transmissions* to replace the friction clutches of the manual transmissions. In the automatic transmission, the gears are shifted automatically when the engine reaches certain speeds, resulting in much easier driving.

The *drive shaft* carries the motive power from the transmission to the *differential*. The drive shaft is connected to the transmission and the differential by one or two *universal joints*. The differential allows the engine's power to turn the drive wheels. When the automobile turns a corner, the differential uses a system of gears to allow the outside wheels to rotate faster than the wheels on the inside. One disadvantage of the differential is its action when the wheels slip, as on ice. If one wheel slips, it will begin to spin rapidly, whereas the other wheel will stand still. Many cars are equipped with a positive traction device to overcome this difficulty. A final drive axle provides a connection between the differential and the wheel hubs.

## STEERING SYSTEMS

A series of gears, rods, and shafts converts the circular motion of the steering wheel to the sideways motion required to turn the wheels when steering. When a car is motionless or moving very slowly, turning the wheels can require considerable force. Most manu-

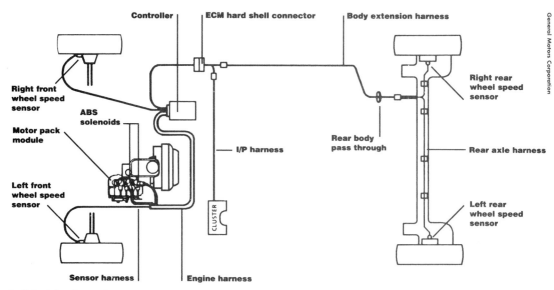

**Anti-lock brake system**

facturers ease the driver's burden by offering what is called *power steering*, a system that applies hydraulic force to the steering mechanism to make turning easier. Some cars have speed-sensitive power steering, which controls the amount of power assist based on how fast the car is moving.

### BRAKE SYSTEMS

Two different methods are used to slow and stop the movement of a car. *Drum brakes* have a metal cylinder attached to each wheel. Around this cylinder, a heavy material called the *shoe* is pushed against the cylinder when pressure is applied to the brake pedal. *Disk brakes* use a metal disk in place of the cylinder. When the brake pedal is pressed, a pair of *pads* are pressed against opposite sides of the disk.

In both drum and disc brakes, *hydraulic*

*brake lines* transfer pressure from the brake pedal to the mechanisms in the wheels. In some automobiles, disc brakes are used on the front wheels, and drum brakes on the rear wheels. Most cars now have *power brakes* that increase the power applied to the brake pedal with power generated by the engine.

### BODY

Concern with speed, safety, economy, and style has caused many changes in automotive design and construction. Streamlined *bodies* reduce wind resistance and increase speed and efficiency. Welded *unit construction* of the body and frame is now used in most cars to increase strength and reduce rattles. More fiberglass and plastic bodies and body parts are made for today's autos.

Automobiles provide smooth, comfortable rides because of their *suspension systems*.

A Saturn SL 2 moves along the assembly line.

These systems are located between the wheels and the frame. A combination of *leaf* and *coil springs* plus *shock absorbers* is used in one common type of system.

### LOOKING BACKWARD AND AHEAD

The first steam-powered automobile was invented in 1769 by the Frenchman Nacelle Cugnot. In 1876, the German engineer Nikolaus Otto built the first, modern gas-powered engine. By the 1890s, inventors in France, Germany, and the U.S. were developing their own forerunners of today's car.

In the 1990s, automobile manufacturers throughout the world are concerned with safety, fuel economy, air pollution, and quality construction. Air bags (to provide protection against frontal collisions) and anti-lock brakes (to prevent tires from skidding on the road) are appearing in more and more cars. Smaller, more efficient engines and lighter cars are helping to squeeze more travelling efficiency out of every drop of gasoline. Unleaded gasoline, engines that recirculate exhaust gases, and catalytic converters that change exhaust gases into harmless vapor help reduce air pollution.     H.P.O./A.J.H./J.H.

SEE ALSO: AIR POLLUTION, AUTOMATION, BATTERY, BRAKES, ENGINE, GENERATOR, PETROLEUM

**Autonomic nervous system** When a child goes to school he may walk fast or slow. He decides at what speed he will go. He uses his legs to walk and arms to carry books. These actions are controlled by decision. There are many things people usually cannot decide. They can't control heart beat. They have difficulty controlling their breathing. Actions over which people have little voluntary control are done automatically by the autonomic nervous system. Now some people are trying to develop control using BIOFEEDBACK.

Along with the control of the rate of the heart beat and breathing, the autonomic (parasympathetic) nervous system governs the contraction of smooth muscles in the skin, digestive tract, the blood vessels, the bladder, and the bronchi of the lungs. It also controls the secretion of various glands. The autonomic system is itself governed by the reflex centers of the central NERVOUS SYSTEM and does not function independently.

---

✳ **THINGS TO DO**

#### CAN YOU STOP YOURSELF FROM DOING THESE ACTIONS?

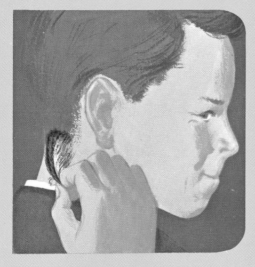

1   Have someone tickle the back of your neck with a feather. Can you stop from having "goose pimples?"

2   When you are embarrassed keep yourself from blushing. Don't permit the blood vessels to dilate in your face which causes the flushed appearance.

3   As you get a strong impulse to sneeze, try to stop it. Do not touch your nose with your hand.

4   All of these responses are reflexes controlled by the autonomic nervous system. They are done automatically and usually out of our control. Can you see the advantage this has for the proper functioning of our bodies?

The autonomic nervous system is divided into two parts: the *sympathetic* division and the *parasympathetic* division. They are basically alike in cellular structure, consisting of bead-like *ganglia* which make connections with the central nervous system and also send out fibers to various parts of the body. These fibers leaving the ganglia differ from ordinary nervous fibers, for they are not covered with a *myelin sheath*. There is always a chain of at least two neurons between the nerve cord and the end organ.

However, the two divisions are located in different areas and are opposite in their action. The parasympathetic system is located in two parts of the body; in the brain (midbrain and medulla) and in the sacral region of the spine. The sympathetic system extends along the thoracic and lumbar regions of the spinal cord. The ganglia are arranged in pairs on each side of the vertebral column.

The autonomic nervous system functions to maintain an internal balance within the various organs of the body. Nerve fibers from both the sympathetic and parasympathetic system affect the same organ. They are opposite in their effect upon the organ. For example, the parasympathetic nerves slow the heart beat; the sympathetic sends impulses to accelerate it. The parasympathetic system causes secretion of the salivary glands, whereas the sympathetic inhibits secretion. Impulses from the parasympathetic cause contraction of the pupil of the eye while the sympathetic sends impulses to dilate the pupil. The behavior of any organ which is controlled by the autonomic nervous system is the net result of the opposing impulses of the parasympathetic and the sympathetic divisions.

The autonomic nervous system releases hormones from its nerve endings. The neurohormones of the sympathetic system are identical in action with adrenalin and parasympathetic nerve endings release acetylcholine.

The autonomic nervous system and its companion, the ADRENAL GLAND, prepare the body to meet situations that present a threat to its normal functioning. The sympathetic system prepares the body for action often called the fright, flight, or fight responses; the parasympathetic system saves the resources of the body.  G.A.D.

SEE ALSO: NERVE CELL, SPINAL CORD

**Autotomy** (awh-TOTE-uh-me) Autotomy is a process in which an animal destroys certain parts of its body in order to escape capture by other animals.

This process is termed *self-mutilation.* Through the presence of special modifications at the base of the appendage or limbs some insects and crustaceans are able to drop these appendages off when another animal seizes them. Some examples of these are the claws of the CRAYFISH, the arms of a STARFISH, and the tails of some lizards.

Autotomy may be followed by *regeneration,* which is the process by which some animals are able to grow new parts of their bodies when old parts are torn off.  V. V. N.

SEE ALSO: ANIMAL, CRUSTACEA, INSECTA, REGENERATION

**Autumn** see Seasons

**Autumnal equinox** The autumnal equinox is the start of autumn. It occurs about September 22 in the northern hemisphere. On this date, DAY AND NIGHT are of equal length and the sun is shining at both poles.

SEE: EQUINOX, SEASONS

**Auxin** see Hormones, plant

**Avalanche** Mountain sides or sloping cliffs may be covered with snow. When the snow is heavy it may begin to slide. This sliding snow is called an *avalanche.* Sometimes this sliding starts when there is a heavy wind or melting. Even small motions can start an avalanche. When the slide goes, it may move slowly or as fast as 100 MPH (161 kph) an hour. Sliding rocks and earth is called a *landslide.*

An avalanche will not take place if the angle of the slope against the ground is less than 25 degrees. If the slant is greater than 35 degrees, and if there is a foot (.3048 meters) of new snow present, an avalanche is likely to occur. Slab avalanches of wind-packed snow are very hazardous.  D.E.Z.

**Aves** see Birds

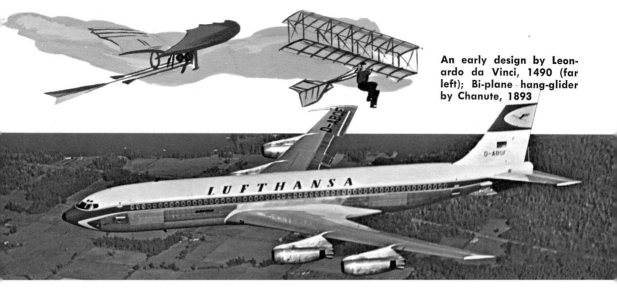

An early design by Leonardo da Vinci, 1490 (far left); Bi-plane hang-glider by Chanute, 1893

**707 Jet airliner carrying more than one hundred passengers**

**Aviation** Aviation is a term used to include all of man's activities concerned with flight through the AT-MOSPHERE. This means aircraft manufacturing, commercial and private flying, as well as all related and supporting activities. A new term, *Aerospace,* is frequently used in place of *aviation,* as it includes man's flight beyond the atmosphere into space.

Aviation, as a mode of transportation, has made a great impact upon human life. It has enabled man to become independent of geographical barriers and to travel swiftly over great distances. Rapid changes in social, political and economic traditions of the world have been brought about. Aviation has had a tremendous influence on international affairs and military concepts.

### EARLY HISTORY

The beginning of aviation is lost in the dim legends of man which tell of flying gods and heroes. The first scientific approach to the problems of flight was made by LEONARDO DA VINCI, of Italy, several hundred years ago. His designs for man-powered flapping wings, HELICOPTERS and PARACHUTES were remarkably far-seeing, yet he had no suitable powerplant, and flew only models of his designs.

For centuries and in many countries, man continued the search for the secrets of flight. Observing the flight of birds revealed valuable knowledge, such as the curved surface of the wing and the advantage of launching into the wind. All efforts failed to successfully develop an *ornithopter* to imitate bird's flapping wings.

The *Montgolfier* brothers in France observed the rising action of warm air and experimented with cloth, hot-air-filled balloons. Man's first successful flight into the atmosphere took place in 1783, beneath one of these BALLOONS. Hydrogen gas soon replaced hot air, making possible extended flights. Another Frenchman, *Henri Giffard,* solved the major problem of directing flight in 1852 by building a streamlined or cigar-shaped DIRIGIBLE balloon which was propelled forward by a lightweight steam engine connected to a propeller.

Although successful flight was achieved with lighter-than-air craft, experiments continued with heavier-than-air craft. Early in the 1800's *Sir George Cayley* of England presented his belief that the solution to flight lay in a fixed curved wing, rather than the flapping type and that the aircraft should be driven with mechanical power. The knowledge Cayley contributed to the science of flight from his glider experiments was so valuable that he has become known as the "father of aeronautics."

Successful glider flights and other experiments by the German Otto Lilienthal and the Americans Octave Chanute, John Montgomery and Samuel Langley, aroused the serious interest of the Wright Brothers in aircraft flight. ORVILLE AND WILBUR WRIGHT scientifically collected as much data as was available and supplemented this knowledge with their own experimenta·

**McDonnell Douglas DC-10**

McDonnell Douglas Corporation

tions. This resulted in the design and perfection of a highly successful glider in 1902 which could be easily controlled in flight. The Wright brothers next developed a suitable light weight engine and effective propeller which were added to their glider. Mythological dreams became a scientific reality on December 17, 1903, as Orville Wright made the first successful powered flight of 12 seconds duration at Kitty Hawk, North Carolina.

## WORLD WAR I AVIATION

The pressure of the First World War brought the airplane out of its infancy into practical use as a weapon. At first, aerial reconnaissance was the primary role of the airplane. As the information brought back by flying scouts became increasingly important to the success of the ground armies, the pursuit plane, with machine guns, was developed to destroy enemy scouts.

Aerial combat was born as the scout airplanes became armed and the aircraft battled each other for control of the sky. Aircraft were developed to attack enemy ground forces with machine guns and crude bombs. Large scale efforts to develop and construct superior aircraft were expended by the opposing governments, providing the impetus for the establishment of a real aircraft manufacturing industry.

## POST WORLD WAR I AVIATION

At the end of World War I, surplus military aircraft were sold to former military pilots and soon "barnstormers" were introducing aviation throughout the country. Aircraft and engine improvements continued. Now speed and altitude records were constantly being set, oceans were spanned and round-the-world flights accomplished.

The Atlantic Ocean was conquered in 1919 by U.S. Navy airmen flying in the Curtiss flying boat NC-4. The organization of official government committees and services provided a stimulus for the aviation industry. A young American, CHARLES A. LINDBERGH, electrified the world in 1927 by flying solo non-stop between New York and Paris. A surge of enthusiasm for flying followed this feat and brought about new support to the infant aviation industry.

In the 1930's the air transport industry took root and began to grow. Airway facilities became adequate for scheduled flight operations. Airlines themselves advanced from converted military biplanes to all-metal, trimotor and twin-engined monoplanes. The famous Ford Trimotor and Douglas D C series of airplanes became familiar sights to air travelers.

## WORLD WAR II AVIATION

Aviation made great advances during World War II. The manufacturing industry expanded to produce over 200,000 aircraft. Accelerated research made possible more powerful engines, new materials, faster and larger aircraft, new electronics and communications equipment, and countless other technological developments which would have perhaps taken decades to bring about in peaceful times. As military aircraft in World War I were an auxiliary aid to the ground forces, World War II air power became a striking force in its own right.

The *turbojet* engine was developed early in World War II, but did not receive wide scale use until after the war. This powerplant is characterized by its light weight, simplicity of operation and ability to deliver tremendous power at high speeds and altitudes. It is ideally suited for aircraft use and has made possible today's high performance jet aircraft.

The first postwar airliners were civilian copies of military transports, such as the Douglas DC-4 and DC-6 and the Lockheed Constellation, powered with conventional

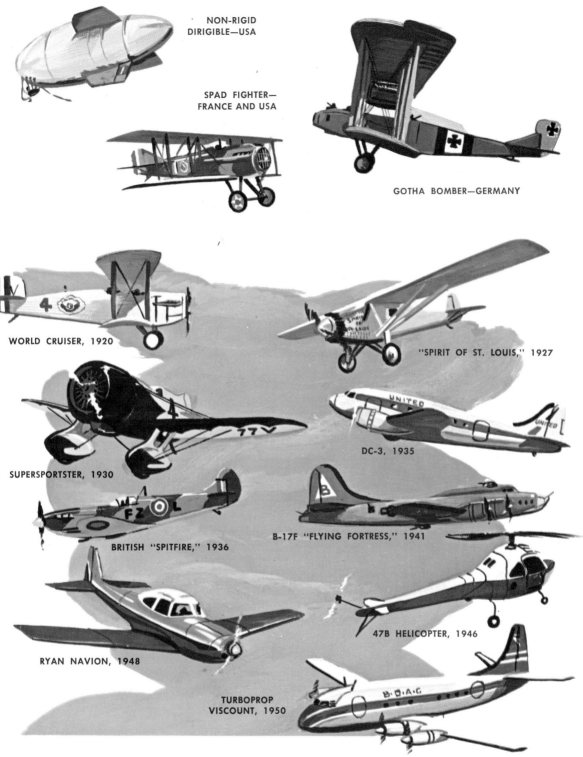

NON-RIGID DIRIGIBLE—USA

SPAD FIGHTER— FRANCE AND USA

GOTHA BOMBER—GERMANY

WORLD CRUISER, 1920

"SPIRIT OF ST. LOUIS," 1927

SUPERSPORTSTER, 1930

DC-3, 1935

BRITISH "SPITFIRE," 1936

B-17F "FLYING FORTRESS," 1941

47B HELICOPTER, 1946

RYAN NAVION, 1948

TURBOPROP VISCOUNT, 1950

piston engines and propellers. Then in 1952 Britain's de Havilland Comet launched the age of commercial jet aviation. The first jet transport in the U.S. was the Boeing 707, which made its initial test flight on July 15, 1954.

In that same year a NACA engineer, Richard T. Whitcomb, discovered a way to reduce drag by giving supersonic military aircraft a "wasp-waist" or "Coke-bottle" shape. It was used in the world's first supersonic bomber, the Convair B-58 *Hustler*.

Shape refinements, along with new wing designs, made propeller-driven airliners virtually obsolete, and soon the world's airlines were re-equipped with pure jet engines that upped their speed close to 600 miles (966 kilometers) per hour.

(Above) Complex cockpit instruments of experimental B-1. (Right) SST Concorde.

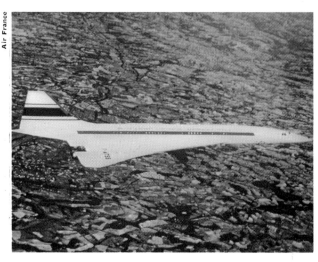

On the drawing boards for the future were hypersonic airliners capable of speeds up to 5,000 miles (8,047 kilometers) per hour, but there seemed to be no practical need for such craft. Instead, the airlines introduced wide-bellied jumbo jets that could carry up to 400 passengers in spacious cabins. Shorter-range passenger jets also began to serve intermediate cities.

In the 1960s the "SST race" was on, with the U.S., Russia, and a joint British-French team in the running. Russia's TU-144 was first to become operational. On April 17, 1966, a TU-144 left Moscow to start nonstop service to Tokyo, an 11-hour run.

The British-French *Concorde* flew next. By 1977 it was undergoing trial flights over the "Blue Ribbon" transatlantic run from London to New York, where opposition developed to its potentially high noise level. (Actually, to avoid the phenomenon called supersonic booms, the *Concorde* SST does not fly supersonically over land.)

The newest trend in commercial aviation is increased reliance on narrow-bodied, two-engine jet planes such as the Boeing 767. Jets that use fuel less efficiently are being phased out of the commercial fleets.

## COMMERCIAL AVIATION TODAY

In August 1992, United Airlines announced it would begin around-the-world flights on February 10, 1993. United One will fly westbound, taking 47 hours to circle the globe, including stops at various international airports. United Two will fly eastbound, taking 39 hours and 41 minutes for the full flight. Around-the-world tickets, if purchased in the United States, each cost between $2,241 for economy class up to $4,159 for first class.

Relatively few people will enjoy the excitement of an earth-circling flight on a single plane. But aviation is an enormous business. The world's busiest airport, Chicago's O'Hare International, was visited by more than 59 million passengers in 1991.

During the year 1990, approximately 500 commercial airlines throughout the world carried about 1.1 billion passengers. Many passengers travelled between cities in a single nation. Others travelled to foreign countries. The world's busiest airport for international travelers is London's Heathrow Airport. It handled more than 33 million international passengers in 1991, compared to 21 million at Charles de Gaulle Aeroport in Paris and just over 10 million at Los Angeles International Airport in the U.S.

For decades, the United States and Western Europe have been leaders in commercial aviation. Some Asian nations have been rapidly catching up. For the past several years, polls of international business fliers indicate that Changi Airport on the island nation of Singapore is the world's finest—and loveliest—airport. Averaging more than 2,200 flights a week in 1992, Changi features sparkling brooks and waterfalls, lighted fountains and gardens, fresh orchids everywhere, fine shops and restaurants, and, perhaps, the world's best service.

Airports are an important part of aviation. They provide refueling and maintenance facilities, flight control and communication equipment and personnel, and everything that is needed to care for passengers and cargo. Runways for large jet airliners approach 2 miles (3.2 km) in length.

Increasing competition and high fuel costs have led many airlines to change their travel routes in recent decades. In the U.S., for example, the government stopped controlling airline ticket prices and routes in 1984. The move forced most carriers to cut costs in order to survive. Many airlines began using what is called "hub-and-spoke" route systems. This strategy allows small airplanes (sometimes propeller-driven models) to deliver passengers to a central airport, where they transfer to larger planes to continue their flights.

**X-15 rocket plane, aircraft with rocket engine that broke all speed records in October, 1961**

KC10-A cargo and troop carrier, completed in 1980, has a wingspan of just over 165 feet (50.4 m). Experimental new aircraft built with Stealth technology are difficult to detect with conventional radar equipment.

## MILITARY AVIATION TODAY

Military aviation refers to the aircraft, airports, air-borne weapons, and support systems that are an important element in the armed forces of the world's nations. Because they are involved in national defense and life-or-death situations, military aircraft are technologically advanced. Many innovations useful for all types of aviation began in the military. They include the invention of the HELICOPTER and JET PROPULSION, the use of RADAR for aircraft identification, and many types of control and navigation equipment.

The largest, fastest, and most expensive aircraft in the aviation world have been developed for military use. Costs are staggering. A U.S. fighter plane, for example, cost a little more than $50,000 to build in 1945. By the late 1980s, development costs for a fighter plane were in the billions of dollars.

A navigational system currently coming into general use in commercial aviation was developed in the military. It is called VOR, which stands for Very-high-frequency Omni-directional Range. A VOR navigation center transmits 360 different signals spaced one degree apart, spreading out much like a bicycle wheel's spokes. The precision signals, coupled with computerized equipment in an aircraft, allows a pilot to follow precise flight paths.

Modern military aircraft serve highly specialized functions. Some of the swiftest can cruise at three times the SPEED OF SOUND. Huge airplanes capable of carrying massive amounts of cargo and hundreds of armed troops have been developed. The huge U.S.

## GENERAL AVIATION TODAY

A huge and sometimes overlooked field, general aviation refers to all aspects of flying not connected with commercial airlines or military aviation. It includes such activities as sport and hobby flying, business flying, police and medical work, crop dusting, forest fire spraying, and so on.

For decades, the United States has led the world in general aviation activity. There are four times as many private airplanes in active service in the U.S. as there are commercial airliners. The U.S. has more than 16,500 general aviation airports used by more than 700,000 private pilots. The busiest general aviation field in the U.S. is California's Van Nuys Airport, owned by the city of Los Angeles. In 1991, approximately 500,000 take-offs and landings were made at Van Nuys.

Private pilots fly aircraft ranging from sleek corporate jets to inexpensive ultralights that fly little faster than an adult can run. Some private pilots belong to flying clubs which allow them to share airplanes with many different people. In the U.S. and most other nations, private pilots must be licensed before they can fly a plane. Earning a pilot's license is both difficult and expensive. Students must pass a series of written exams testing many different areas of knowledge. Usually, they must also pay for classroom time and for instructors and airplane rentals while practicing in the air.

In recent years, the skies around major cities have become increasingly congested by

Don Dwiggins Photo

USAF Photo

(Left) The VariEze craft uses the Whitcomb Winglet. (Right) Black Bart broke speed records.

air traffic. In some cases, private pilots have interfered with commercial airliners and military flights. Methods of controlling air traffic in urban areas, without unduly restricting general aviation, are still being developed.

### FLIGHT SAFETY

Despite increasingly crowded skies, studies have shown airplane travel to be safer than travel by automobile. In most nations of the world, government agencies play an active role ensuring that aviation remains safe.

In Western Europe, governments must work together closely to ensure safety, since distances between nations are not great. Private enterprise cooperates as well. A number of highly successful airliners have been developed by a five-nation European conglomeration called Airbus Industrie. In European nations and most other countries, government bureaucrats work with private industry to develop safety standards. Those standards affect the licensing of pilots, mechanics, traffic controllers, and other critical personnel, aircraft manufacturing specifications, maintenance procedures, flight patterns, airport facilities, and much more. The United Nation's International Civil Aviation Organization (ICAO) sets standards to ensure that navigation equipment and flight routes are coordinated internationally. The navigation system used by all international flights is called Omega. The system broadcasts navigational signals from eight different sites scattered around the world.

In the United States, all aspects of air traffic and aviation safety are governed by the Federal Aviation Administration (FAA). The FAA also investigates accidents. Great care is taken to determine the cause of every serious accident. Most commercial airliners today carry voice and data recorders popularly called "black boxes." Designed to survive even serious crashes, the devices record cockpit conversations and critical instrument readings. In the event of a crash, a black box will often help to reveal what went wrong.

Since the 1960s, one of the most serious safety hazards faced by the world's commercial airlines involves international terrorism. Most airports have now installed X-RAY equipment to detect weapons and explosives carried by passengers or in cargo. The efforts have lessened, but not eliminated, the danger of crimes being committed aboard commercial airplanes.

### THE FUTURE OF AVIATION

The future offers both problems to solve and opportunities to explore. Growing numbers of air travellers will require greater efforts to reduce congestion and noise and air pollution in urban areas. The petroleum used to make aviation fuel is not limitless. New types of fuel and more efficient engines may have to be developed.

But the future also may bring great innovations. New designs for airplanes may begin to merge with rocket science. In the future, aircraft may travel to the brink of space, reaching the farthest points on earth in just two hours or so. At the same time, aircraft capable of landing and taking off vertically may drastically change the nature of airports and the distances people must travel to reach them. All the while, aviators will be working to make flying in the sky safer, cleaner, faster, more fuel-efficient, and more fun than ever before. D.D./R.J.J./J.H.

SEE ALSO: AERODYNAMICS; AERONAUTICS; AIRCRAFT; AIRPLANE; AIRSHIP; ASTRONAUTICS; ELECTRONICS; FLIGHT, PRINCIPLES OF; INSTRUMENT LANDING SYSTEM; INSTRUMENT PANEL; JET PROPULSION; ROCKET ENGINE; SPACE TRAVEL; SPACE VEHICLES

**Avocado** (av-uh-KAH-doh) Avocado is an evergreen tree and the fruit that grows on it. It is also called *alligator pear*. It belongs to the LAUREL family. It grows in California, Florida, southern Mexico, and Central America.

The tree will grow to 50 feet (15.2 meters) tall in the wild state. In orchards, the height is kept about 30 feet (9.1 meters) for easy harvesting. The wood is not sturdy, so avocados are not planted in regions of strong winds. Since it cannot withstand freezing, its cultivation is limited to tropical areas. The leaves are long.

The ground or oval FRUIT can develop up to 9 inches (23 centimeters) long and weight 2 pounds (.91 kilograms). The tough skin may be green to black in color. The pulp or *mesocarp* is yellow and has a very delicate taste. It is rich in vitamins, has a higher percentage of protein than most fruits, and has from 5% to 30% fat. It is classified as a one-seeded BERRY. The fruit ripens after it is picked for market. H.J.C.

**Avocets are shore birds**

**Avocet** (AV-uh-set) The avocet is one of a group of birds that live along the shore of lakes, ponds, and rivers. Avocets are found in warm and temperate climates of both the eastern and western hemispheres. They have webbed feet, long legs, and a slender bill that curves upward toward the end. They wade, swim, dive, fly, and have loud, noisy, yelping voices.

The American avocet is partially tan and has distinctive black and white marks. It is found from southwestern Canada to Mexico and Guatemala. Plants, small water animals, and insects—including some that are harmful to man—make up the diet of this bird. The male and female take turns sitting on and protecting the eggs of their offspring. J. D. B.

**Avogadro's Law** see Gas

**Avoirdupois system** see Measurement, Weight

**Axillary** see Bud

**Axle** see Machines, simple

**Axon** see Nerve cell

**Azalea** (uh-ZAYL-yuh) This is a small to large flowering shrub. The leaves are simple and leathery. They are often hairy with smooth edges. The flowers are usually white, pink, orange, or purple.

Azalea plants range in height from 3 to 20 feet (.91 to 6.1 meters). Most of them are deciduous (dropping their leaves before winter) but a few are evergreen (staying on all winter). The leaves and buds grow near the end of the twig. The lateral buds develop into leaves and the terminal bud usually produces the flower.

Azaleas are related to the RHODODENDRON. They thrive in acid soil with an average $pH$ of 5.0. Azaleas are attacked by a flower blight in hot, humid areas of the country. Between infection periods, this parasite lies dormant in the soil in hard coverings. P.G.B.

SEE ALSO: RHODODENDRON

# Conversion Factors
# to Metric Measurement

### Length
1 inch = 25.4 millimeters (mm) exactly
1 inch = 2.54 centimeters (cm) exactly
1 foot = 0.3048 meters (m) exactly
1 yard = 0.9144 meters (m) exactly
1 mile = 1.609344 kilometers (km) exactly

### Area
1 square inch = 6.4516 square centimeters ($cm^2$) exactly
1 square foot = 0.092903 square meters ($m^2$)
1 square yard = 0.836127 square meters ($m^2$)
1 square acre = 0.404686 hectares (ha)
1 square mile = 2.58999 square kilometers ($km^2$)

### Cubic Measure
1 cubic inch = 16.387064 cubic centimeters ($cm^3$) exactly
1 cubic foot = 0.0283168 cubic meters ($m^3$)
1 cubic yard = 0.764555 cubic meters ($m^3$)

### US Liquid Measure
1 fluid ounce = 29.5735 milliliters (ml)
1 fluid ounce = 0.2957 deciliters (dl)
1 pint = 0.473176 liters (l)
1 gallon = 3.78541 liters (l)

### US Dry Measure
1 pint = 0.550610 liters (l)
1 bushel = 35.2391 liters (l)

### Weight
1 grain = 0.0647989 grams (g)
1 ounce = 28.3495 grams (g)
1 pound = 0.453592 kilograms (kg)
1 short ton = 0.907185 metric tons (t)
1 UK ton = 1.01605 metric tons (t)

### Temperature
To convert Fahrenheit to Centigrade complete the following equation.
$$(F° - 32) \times 5 \div 9 = C°$$